Homework
Workbook

Grade 6

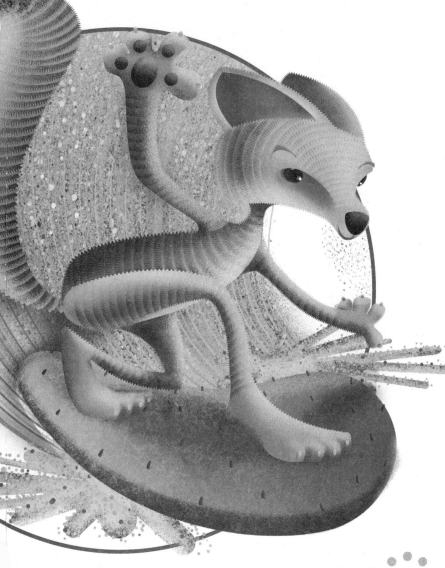

Scott Foresman·Addison Wesley

enVisionMATH™

Scott Foresman
is an imprint of

pearsonschool.com

Editorial Offices: Glenview, Illinois • Parsippany, New Jersey • New York, New York
Sales Offices: Boston, Massachusetts • Duluth, Georgia • Glenview, Illinois
Coppell, Texas • Sacramento, California • Mesa, Arizona

ISBN – 13: 978-0-328-34179-5

ISBN – 10: 0-328-34179-7

11 12 13 14   V0N4   15 14 13

Table of Contents

Place Value

For **1–4**, write the place and the value of the underlined digit.

1. 20<u>5</u>,300,005,001 _____

2. <u>6</u>80,525,917,143 _____

3. 10<u>2</u>,105,000,071,000 _____

4. 40,400,0<u>4</u>0,000,444 _____

5. Write the number 100,050,000,982 in expanded form using only addition.

_____

_____

6. What is 23,000,400,000,158 in word form?

   A Twenty-three million, four hundred thousand, one hundred fifty-eight

   B Twenty-three billion, four hundred million, one hundred fifty-eight

   C Twenty-three trillion, four hundred million, one hundred fifty-eight

   D Two trillion, three billion, four million, one hundred fifty-eight

7. **Algebra** A megabyte holds about 1,000,000 characters of data.
   A gigabyte holds about 1,000 times more data than a megabyte.
   About how many characters of data does the gigabyte hold?

   A One trillion

   B One billion

   C One million

   D One thousand

8. **Writing to Explain** How are the labels in each period alike? How are they different?

_____

_____

_____

_____

Comparing and Ordering Whole Numbers

Use < or > to compare.

1. 9,035 ◯ 9,062   **2.** 362,286 ◯ 360,055   **3.** 7,261,005 ◯ 7,266,500

For **4** and **5,** order the numbers from least to greatest.

4. 75,321; 72,369; 72,752; 57,575

_____

5. 6,074,232; 6,234,921; 6,243,219

_____

For **6** and **7,** order from greatest to least.

6. 300 thousand; 300 billion; 3 trillion; 30 million

_____

7. 4,810,414; 4,767,894; 4,562,626; 4,909,000

_____

8. Writing to Explain Tell how you would decide if 9,899,989 is greater than or less than 9,898,998.

_____

_____

9. Number Sense If you plot these numbers on a number line, which one will be in the middle? 105,394; 150,494; 115,054

_____

10. Geometry Which of these figures has the greatest perimeter?

   A A square with sides 109 meters long

   B A hexagon with sides 65 meters long

   C A rectangle with length 24 meters and width 46 meters

   D A pentagon with sides 72 meters long

Exponents and Place Value

Write each expression in exponential form.

1. $5 \times 5 \times 5 \times 5 \times 5 \times 5$ _____

2. $2 \times 2 \times 2 \times 2 \times 2 \times 2 \times 2$ _____

3. $3 \times 3 \times 3$ _____

4. 9 _____

Write each number in expanded form using exponents.

5. 53,806 _____

6. 527,519 _____

Evaluate.

7. 6^2 _____

8. 5^3 _____

9. 3^6 _____

10. 2^8 _____

11. Reasoning Zach invested $50 and was able to triple his money in two years. Kayla also began with $50 in investments, and was able to cube her money in two years. Who had more money after two years? Explain.

_____

_____

_____

12. Writing to Explain In 1968, the estimated population of the world was 3,559,028,982 people. When this number is written in expanded form using exponents, one power of 10 would not be represented. Which power of 10? Why?

_____

_____

13. Number Sense Which is **NOT** equal to 1?

    A 10^0

    B 4^1

    C 1×10^0

    D 1^4

Decimal Place Value

Write the place and value of the underlined digit.

1. 56.3<u>8</u>9 _____

2. 9.643<u>7</u>2 _____

Write the number given in the form indicated.

3. 8.7204 in expanded form _____

4. 43 and 962 ten thousandths in standard form _____

What is the whole number portion of the decimal?

5. 5.024 _____

6. 418.0972 _____

What is the decimal portion of the decimal?

7. 176.261 _____

8. 91.0213 _____

The slowest growing tree is a White Cedar in Canada. It grew about 0.0658 centimeters per year in 155 years. Use this information to answer **9** and **10.**

9. To what decimal place value is the yearly growth measured?

_____

10. How would you write this number in word form?

_____

11. Number Sense Write a decimal that has 6 in the hundredths place and the ten-thousandths place. _____

12. Writing to Explain How would you write a decimal that is less than 5 ten-thousandths?

_____

_____

13. Which shows the short-word form for 16.011?

    A 16 and 11 thousandths

    B 16 and 11 ten-thousandths

    C 16 and 11 hundredths

    D 16 and 11 tenths

4

Multiplying and Dividing by 10, 100, and 1,000

Find each product or quotient.

1. 0.006 × 10 = _____

2. 0.64 ÷ 10 = _____

3. 123.3 ÷ 100 = _____

4. 8.7 × 100 = _____

5. 0.145 × 1,000 = _____

6. 542.3 ÷ 1,000 = _____

7. 0.91 × 100 = _____

8. 0.1 ÷ 10 = _____

9. 100 ÷ 1,000 = _____

10. 2 ÷ 100 = _____

11. 0.302 × 1,000 = _____

12. 1.397 × 100 = _____

13. 0.038 ÷ 10 = _____

14. 0.0115 × 10 = _____

15. Reasoning What number do you need to multiply by 100 to get the same result as 16.2 ÷ 10? Explain.

_____

_____

16. Number Sense An alligator hatchling grew to 72.5 inches after six years. This length is 10 times its hatchling length. If you want to know its hatchling length, should you multiply or divide 72.5 by 10? Explain.

_____

_____

17. What is the quotient of 12.12 ÷ 100?

   A 0.1212

   B 1.212

   C 121.2

   D 1,212

18. Writing to Explain Casey said that 0.03 × 1,000 is 3. Explain why Casey's answer is not correct. What mistake do you think he made?

_____

_____

Name _____

Comparing and Ordering Decimals

Use >, <, or = to compare each pair of numbers.

1. 656.07 ◯ 656.23

2. 73.42 ◯ 72.56

3. 0.01 ◯ 0.10

4. 7.999 ◯ 7.998

Order from least to greatest.

5. 639.087, 639.078, 639.088

_____

6. 0.0909, 0.0989, 0.0999

_____

7. Geometry Which circle has the greatest circumference? How do you know?

4.25 in.

A

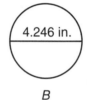
4.246 in.

B

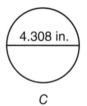
4.308 in.

C

_____

_____

8. Writing to Explain How would you find a number between 3.2 and 3.26?

_____

_____

9. Which decimal is greater than 3.33 but less than 3.34?

    A 2.3349

    B 3.305

    C 3.329

    D 3.336

Problem Solving: Make an Organized List

Solve by making an organized list. The lists have been started for you. Complete the lists and answer the questions.

1. A balloon game at the county fair gives 1,000 points, 500 points, and 250 points for each balloon that you pop. If Stewart buys 2 darts, how many possible points can he score?

1,000	500	250	Total
✓ ✓			2,000
✓	✓		1,500
✓		✓	1,250

_____

2. How many different 3-letter combinations can you make with the letters, L, G, and F?

L	G	F
LGF		
LFG		

_____

3. In a chess tournament, Miguel, Rebecca, Kyle, Ana, and Josh will play each other once. How many games will they play?

M	R	K	A	J
MR				
MK				
MA				
MJ				

_____

4. Tanya has to wear a cap and T-shirt for her job at the amusement park. She can wear a red, blue, or yellow cap and a red or green shirt. How many different cap and shirt pairs can Tanya wear?

A 5   **B** 6   **C** 9   **D** 10

5. **Writing to Explain** How could you find the number of different combinations of 6 letters in a computer password?

Using Variables to Write Expressions

Write each algebraic expression.

1. 6 more than a number c _____

2. twice a number b _____

3. 25 less than a number d _____

4. the product of 7 and a number e _____

5. 50 divided by a number f _____

6. the sum of a number g and 2 _____

7. 8 more stripes than a number h _____

8. 12 fewer hats than four times a number i _____

9. Alexander has \$10. He buys a snack. Which expression shows how much money Alexander has left?

    A $s + 10$

    B $10 - s$

    C $10s$

    D $s \div 10$

10. A diner has booths and counter seating. Each booth can seat 4 people. Another 15 people can sit at the counter. Which expression shows how many customers can be seated in the diner?

    A $15b - 4$

    B $15b + 4$

    C $4b - 15$

    D $4b + 15$

11. **Reasonableness** Linnia bought some flats of flowers. Each flat holds 9 flowers. Linnia has planted 10 flowers. Is $9x + 10$ a reasonable way to represent the number of flowers that Linnia has left to plant? Explain your answer.

_____

_____

_____

Properties of Operations

Find each missing number. Tell what property or properties are shown.

1. (32 + _____) + 2 + 7 = 32 + (14 + 2) + 7

   _____

2. 8 + 6 + 12 = _____ + 12 + 6

   _____

3. (8 × _____) × 7 = 8 × (9 × 7)

   _____

4. _____ + 0 = 34

   _____

5. 12 × 3 = 3 × _____

   _____

6. 1 × _____ = 288

   _____

7. **Reasoning** Write a number sentence that shows why the associative property does not work with subtraction.

   _____

8. Which property is shown in (23 × 5) × 13 × 7 = 23 × (5 × 13) × 7?

   A Commutative Property of Multiplication   **B** Identity Property of Multiplication

   C Associative Property of Multiplication   **D** Associative Property of Addition

9. **Writing to Explain** Explain why you do not have to do any computing to solve 15 × 0 × (13 + 7).

   _____

   _____

Name _____

Order of Operations

Evaluate each expression.

1. $3 + 4 \times 7$

2. $88 - 6 \times 6$

3. $8 \times 2 + 7 \times 3$

_____

_____

_____

4. $(5 + 9) + 3 \times 8$

5. $(6 + 3^2) + 5$

6. $9^2 - (7 \times 5) + 3$

_____

_____

_____

7. $48 \div 2 + 6$

8. $26 \div (5 + 8) + 1$

9. $18 + 3 \times (6 \div 2)$

_____

_____

_____

10. Reasoning What operation would you perform *last* in this problem: $(2 \times 3) + (7 \times 2)$?

_____

Use parentheses to make each number sentence true.

11. $10 + 5 \times 4^2 \div 2^3 = 20$

12. $124 - 6 \times 0 + 15 = 34$

13. $10^2 - 10 + 3 = 93$

14. $7 + 5 \times 3 \div 3 = 12$

15. Mr. Miller's sixth-grade class went on a field trip to hear the symphony perform. Their seats were grouped in the following ways: 2 groups of 3 seats; 3 groups of 4 seats, 4 groups of 2 seats, and 1 seat (for Mr. Miller). Write a number sentence to calculate how many students went on the field trip.

_____

_____

16. Evaluate the expression $(4^2 - 4) + 6 \div 2$.

   A 4   **B** 9   **C** 12   **D** 15

17. Writing to Explain Suppose you had to evaluate $9^2 + 5 \times 4$. Tell the order in which you would compute these numbers.

_____

_____

Name _____

The Distributive Property

Find each missing number.

1. $8 \times (30 + 2) = (8 \times$ _____$) + (8 \times 2)$ **2.** $8(94) = 8($_____$) + 8(4)$

3. $5(45 + 5) = 5($_____$)$ **4.** $9(42) - 9(4) = 9(30) + 9($_____$)$

Use the distributive property and mental math to evaluate.

5. $3(58 - 8)$ _____   **6.** $7(31 + 19)$ _____

7. $9(72)$ _____   **8.** $4(26) - 4(16)$ _____

9. $8(41) + 8(5)$ _____   **10.** $5(22 - 5)$ _____

11. Writing to Explain Describe the mental math steps you would use to find $7(42)$.

_____

_____

12. Number Sense Use mental math to evaluate the expression $6(31) + 6(4) - 6(15)$.

_____

13. Geometry Write an expression for the area of this rectangle.
Evaluate your expression to find the area.

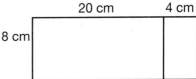

_____

14. Algebra Which expression is equal to $12m + 12n$?

   A $12mn$

   B $12m + n$

   C $12m - 12n$

   D $12(m + n)$

Mental Math

Compute mentally.

1. $8 \times 15 \times 50 =$ _____

2. $634 - 519 =$ _____

3. $78 + 89 =$ _____

4. $37 + 66 + 24 =$ _____

5. $4,922 - 301 =$ _____

6. $7 \times 20 \times 4 =$ _____

7. $34 + 45 + 84 =$ _____

8. $8 \times 8 \times 50 =$ _____

9. Reasoning Explain the steps you can use to find $2 \times 36 \times 50$ mentally.

_____

_____

An apartment complex needs to purchase several new appliances. They have made a price list showing the cost of a few of these appliances. Compute mentally.

Appliance	Price
Refrigerator/freezer	$938
Washing machine	$465
Dryer	$386

10. Find the cost of a washing machine and a dryer.

_____

11. How much more does a refrigerator/ freezer cost than a dryer?

_____

12. Find the total cost for 3 refrigerator/freezers.

_____

13. Compute mentally: $450 - 280$.

    A 120   **B** 140   **C** 170   **D** 190

14. Writing to Explain Explain in your own words why $204 \times 6 = (6 \times 200) + (6 \times 4)$.

_____

_____

_____

_____

Evaluating Expressions

Apply the substitutions and evaluate.

1. $7x - 4$; $x = 9$ **2.** $3d + (5 - d)$; $d = 4$ **3.** $8 + 2g - g \div 2$; $g = 6$

_____   _____   _____

For **7–10**, evaluate each expression for 2, 6, and 8.

4. $5x$ ____, ____, ____   **5.** $x + 12$ ____, ____, ____

6. $96 \div x$ ____, ____, ____   **7.** $x^2 - x$ ____, ____, ____

8. Evaluate the expression for the values of h.

h	6	18	24	42	54
$(h - 6) + h \div 6$					

9. The table shows how much Tia charges for pet sitting. Write an expression to show how much Tia will earn for sitting two dogs for a day and two cats per hour. Then solve for sitting two dogs for the day and one cat for 6 hours.

Number of Pets	Per Day	Per Hour
One dog	$20	$7
Two dogs	$25	$9
One or two cats	$15	$6

_____

10. Writing to Explain Tia wrote $20 + 7x$ to find how much she earned for one pet sitting job and $15x$ for another job. Explain the difference between the expressions.

_____

_____

_____

_____

11. Evaluate the expression $6 + 8f$ for $f = 4$.

     A 8

     B 18

     C 38

     D 56

Using Expressions to Describe Patterns

Use this table for **1–4.**

Total Cups in Boxes	18	36	54	66	72	84
Total Number of Boxes	3	6	9	☐	☐	☐

1. How many boxes are needed for 66, 72, and 84 cups? _____

2. How many cups will be in 20 boxes? _____

3. Write an algebraic expression that explains the relationship between the input (total cups in boxes) and output (total number of boxes) values if the variable *c* is the input. _____

4. **Writing to Explain** Jason thinks he needs 25 boxes to pack 144 cups. Is Jason correct? Explain.

_____

_____

5. **Make a Table** Lily is using seashells to make necklaces. Each necklace has 7 shells. Make an input/output table that shows the number of shells used for 10, 15, 20, and 25 necklaces. Write an algebraic expression that explains the relationship between the input and output values.

Use this table for **6 and 7.**

Large White Butterfly Wing Beats					
Number of seconds	1	2	3	4	5
Number of beats	12	24	36	48	60

6. **Critical Thinking** What algebraic expression shows the number of wing beats for a chosen number of seconds?

   A $60 + x$ **B** $x \div 12$ **C** $12 \div x$ **D** $12x$

7. How many times will a large white butterfly beat its wings in 12 seconds?

   A 144 **B** 120 **C** 84 **D** 72

Problem Solving: Make a Table

1. Selena earns $8.75 per hour working at her job. It costs $3.50 to ride the bus to and from work. Write an expression that describes how much Selena has each day after x hours of work and paying her bus fare.

_____

2. Complete the table to find how much Selena earns each day if she works 3 hours, 5 hours, or 8 hours.

x	
3	
5	
8	

3. A health food store sells protein powder online. A 10-lb carton of protein powder costs $27.25. It costs $4.95 to ship the powder whether you buy 1 or more cartons. Write an expression to show the cost including shipping of x cartons of protein powder.

_____

4. Complete the table to find how much it costs to have 2, 5, and 9 cartons of protein powder shipped.

x	
2	
5	
9	

5. **Critical Thinking** Lee earns 3 points for every dollar he spends at the pet store. Which value completes this table?

x	$3x$
27	?

A 9   **B** 24   **C** 30   **D** 81

6. **Writing to Explain** A wildlife park charges $18 for each admission ticket x. Explain the labels you would use to make a table to find the cost of 4 tickets, 9 tickets, and 12 tickets.

_____

Name _____

Estimating Sums and Differences

Fill in the blanks to complete the estimate.

1. 4.36 − 2.971 =

_____ − 3 = _____

2. 9.384 + 7.713 =

9 + _____ = _____

3. 8.81 + 2.78 =

8.8 + _____ = _____

Round each number to the nearest whole number to estimate the answer.

4. 15.63 − 8.497 _____

5. 3.504 + 7.118 _____

6. 13.09 − 10.902 _____

7. 14.52 + 11.118 _____

8. 9.573 − 4.817 _____

9. 22.174 + 18.561 _____

10. 37.624 − 14.826 _____

11. 15.938 + 7.627 _____

12. 19.394 − 6.943 _____

Round each number to the nearest tenth to estimate the answer.

13. 7.349 + 8.192 _____

14. 14.087 − 5.418 _____

15. 8.991 + 3.475 _____

16. 25.183 − 13.984 _____

17. 11.004 + 5.391 _____

18. 31.038 − 12.861 _____

19. **Geometry** Estimate the perimeter of the figure to the nearest whole number. _____

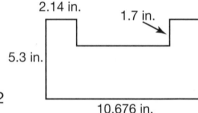

2.14 in.

1.7 in.

5.3 in.

10.676 in.

20. Four runners ran the relay. Bill ran his lap in 22.738 seconds, Tory ran in 21.874 seconds, Grace ran in 20.32 seconds, and Jessica ran in 19.047 seconds. Estimate the team's total time to the nearest tenth of a second.

_____

21. LuWanda bought a jar of mustard, a half-gallon of ice cream, and two boxes of popcorn. She gave the clerk a $20 bill. Estimate how many dollars she received in change.

On Sale Today
Mustard $1.58
Ice cream . . . $3.27
Popcorn $2.19

A $4 **B** $9 **C** $11 **D** $14

22. **Writing to Explain** The digit 5 is usually rounded up, but it can also be rounded down. How would you round the numbers in the equation 9.5 + 4.7 + 3.2 + 7.5 = x to the nearest whole number without getting an overestimate or an underestimate?

_____

_____

_____

Adding and Subtracting

Find each sum or difference.

1. 10.21 − 4.6

_____

2. 0.03 + 1.85

_____

3. 5.011 + 1.23

_____

4. 22.9 − 0.61

_____

5. 9.834 − 1.26

_____

6. 24 + 7.45

_____

7. Complete the sequence of numbers. 4.25, 5, 5.75, _____, _____

8. Number Sense How does the cost for 1 tube of glue compare to the cost for 1 roll of tape?

_____

9. What is the difference in cost between 2 packs of markers and 4 sheets of poster board?

_____

Craft Supplies	
Poster board	$1.29/sheet
Markers	$4.50/pack
Tape	$1.99/roll
Glue	$2.39/tube
Construction paper	$3.79/pack

10. In a long jump competition, Khaila jumped 3.9 meters. Alicia jumped 3.08 meters. How much farther did Khaila jump?

  A 0.01 meters

  B 0.82 meters

  C 0.98 meters

  D 1.01 meters

11. Writing to Explain Trey wrote 9.009 − 0.01 = 9.008. Is his answer correct? Why or why not?

_____

_____

Estimating Products and Quotients

Estimate each answer using rounding.

1. 3.48 × 9.673 _____
2. 5.702 × 4.26 _____
3. 9.734 × 6.8 _____
4. 8.37 × 2.501 _____
5. 7.936 × 2.491 _____
6. 5.092 × 3.774 _____
7. 12.123 × 4.802 _____
8. 6.98 × 8.502 _____
9. 1.948 × 3.728 _____

Estimate each answer using compatible numbers.

10. 19.18 ÷ 3.7
11. 14.9 ÷ 8.432
12. 31.047 ÷ 4.492

13. 16.07 ÷ 4.989
14. 46.614 ÷ 9.01
15. 61.503 ÷ 8.041

16. 73.196 ÷ 11.513
17. 123.82 ÷ 25.937
18. 86.431 ÷ 6.722

19. **Number Sense** An airliner is 9.34 feet wide. The airline wants to install 5 seats in each row. The seats are each 1.46 feet wide. Rounded to the nearest, tenth, about how much space would be left for the aisle? _____

20. **Geometry** Estimate the area of the rectangle. _____

7.278 ft | 13.713 ft

21. **Writing to Explain** The library has a bookshelf 46.725 inches wide for their new encyclopedia. When the encyclopedia arrived, the librarian found that each of the 24 volumes was 1.65 inches wide. Estimate if the 24 books will fit on the shelf. How does your rounding affect the answer?

_____

_____

_____

22. **Algebra** Dominick wants to buy 2 CDs for $14.95 each, 3 DVDs for $19.99 each, and a video game for $36.79. Which equation could you use to estimate how much money he needs?

A 15 + 20 + 26 = x

B 2(14) + 3(20) + 36 = x

C 2(15) + 3(20) + 37 = x

D 2(15) + 3(19) + 36 = x

18

Name _____

Multiplying Decimals

Place the decimal point in each product.

1. 3 × 6.892 = 20676 _____   **2.** 0.3 × 4.57 = 1371 _____

Find each product.

3. 14.3 × 2.1 × 8.9 = _____   **4.** 0.45 × 0.01 = _____

5. 67.1 × 0.3 × 0.4 = _____   **6.** 582.1 × 4.2 = _____

7. Reasoning Show how to find the product of 16.2 × 4 using addition.

_____

8. Which activity is 6 times faster than the fastest rowing speed?

_____

9. The fastest speed a table tennis ball has been hit is 21.12 times faster than the speed for the fastest swimmer. What is the speed for the table tennis ball?

_____

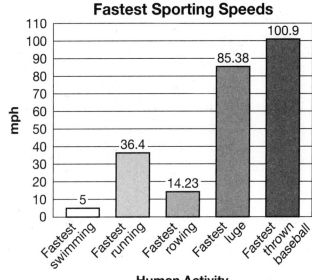

Fastest Sporting Speeds

10. How fast would 1.5 times the fastest rowing speed be?

_____

11. Which is the product of 241.82 × 3.8?

 A 91.8916   **B** 918.916   **C** 9,189.16   **D** 91,891.6

12. Writing to Explain Explain why multiplying 37.4 × 0.01 gives a product that is less than 37.4.

_____

_____

_____

Dividing by a Whole Number

Find the quotient.

1. $42.78 ÷ 3   **2.** 85.5 ÷ 6   **3.** 3.4 ÷ 10

_____   _____   _____

4. 9 ÷ 900   **5.** 59.6 ÷ 8   **6.** 188.4 ÷ 60

_____   _____   _____

7. $1.24 ÷ 4   **8.** 231 ÷ 42   **9.** 11.2 ÷ 25

_____   _____   _____

10. Yolanda bought 8 tickets to a concert for $214. What was the cost
of each ticket?

_____

11. Algebra Tony bought a 72-ounce box of dog biscuits.
How many pounds of dog biscuits did he buy?
(Remember: 1 pound = 16 ounces.)

    A 4 pounds

    B 4.5 pounds

    C 90 pounds

    D 4,320 pounds

12. Number Sense Vicky uses 42 beads for each necklace she
makes. She bought a bag of 500 beads. How many necklaces can
she make?

_____

13. Writing to Explain In what place is the first digit of the quotient for
12.88 ÷ 4? Tell how you know.

_____

_____

Name _____

Practice
3-6

Dividing a Whole Number by a Decimal

Find each quotient. Show your work.

1. $0.7\overline{)84}$ _____

2. $0.3\overline{)123}$ _____

3. $0.005\overline{)281}$ _____

4. $0.007\overline{)287}$ _____

5. $0.006\overline{)135}$ _____

6. $0.08\overline{)28}$ _____

7. $453 \div 0.06$ _____

8. $315 \div 0.9$ _____

9. $516 \div 0.03$ _____

10. $827 \div 0.002$ _____

11. $45 \div 0.0015$ _____

12. $1,233 \div 0.009$ _____

13. A 21-pound turkey was cooked for a small banquet. The caterer figures they will discard 6 pounds of bones and that each person will eat 0.6 pounds of the remaining turkey. How many people will the turkey serve?

_____

14. During a regular half-hour TV show, there are 8 minutes of commercials. If each commercial is 0.25 minutes long, how many commercials will be shown during that show?

_____

15. A machine in a deli cooks hot dogs by rotating them past a heat source. One rotation takes 0.75 minutes, and it takes 9 minutes to fully cook the hot dog. How many rotations does it take to cook the hot dog?

A 8   **B** 9   **C** 11   **D** 12

16. One pound of horsehair is divided into "pulls" to make horsehair belts. One "pull" weighs about 0.011 ounces. How many "pulls" could be made from 3 pounds of horsehair?

_____

17. **Writing to Explain** When you divide a whole number by a decimal less than 1, the quotient is greater than the whole number. Why?

_____

_____

Dividing Decimals

Find each quotient.

1. 8.4 ÷ 0.3 = _____

2. 66.15 ÷ 0.63 = _____

3. 10.5 ÷ 1.5 = _____

4. 86 ÷ 0.4 = _____

5. 72.8 ÷ 1.4 = _____

6. 14.36 ÷ 0.4 = _____

7. 2.87 ÷ 0.01 = _____

8. 78.32 ÷ 0.22 = _____

9. Reasoning Why would multiplying both the dividend and the divisor by 10 sometimes make a problem easier to solve?

_____

_____

For each item, find how many times greater the 2002 cost is than the 1960 cost. Round your answer to the nearest hundredth.

Item	1960 Cost	2002 Cost
Movie admission	$0.75	$8.50
Regular popcorn	$0.25	$3.25
Regular drink	$0.35	$2.75

10. movie admission

11. regular popcorn

12. regular drink

_____   _____   _____

13. Which item has increased the greatest amount of times from its original cost? _____

14. Divide. Round to the nearest hundredth. 250.6 ÷ 1.6

    A 156

    B 156.6

    C 156.61

    D 156.63

15. Writing to Explain Lynn and Randi got different quotients when they divided 3.60 by 0.12. Whose work is correct? Explain why.

                                        Lynn   Randi

                                     0.30   30.0

                                 12)3.60   12)360.

_____

_____

Name _____

Evaluating Expressions

1. $6^2 - (3.1 \times 5 + 2.3)$ **2.** $[(8 - 3.7) \times 6] + 1.5$ **3.** $9^2 - [(4.2 \times 3.4) - 9.28]$

_____ _____ _____

4. $3.2^2 - [(12.6 - 2^2) \times 0.6]$ **5.** $[(0.3 \times 8) + (1.5 \times 3)] + 6^2$

_____ _____

6. $40 \div [9.6 - (8 \times 0.2)]$ **7.** $3^3 + 4.2 \times 8 \div 0.2$

_____ _____

8. $8.8 + [(0.4 \times 7) + (3.1 \times 2)]$ **9.** $7^2 - [(6^2 - 22.4) + (8 \div 0.5)] + 3.8$

_____ _____

10. $9 + [(4.2 - 3.3) + (6.4 \div 0.8)] \times 3$ **11.** $41 - 3^2 + (8 \times 2.3) - 15 + (2.1 \times 4)$

_____ _____

12. $13 + 26 - [(2.8 \times 5) \div 7]$ **13.** $16 + 23 - [(5 + 2) \times 1.9] - 13 + 6.8$

_____ _____

14. Jessica bought a new computer for $800. She put $120 down and got a student discount of $50. Her mother gave her $\frac{1}{2}$ of the balance for her birthday. Which of these expressions could be used to find the amount Jessica still owes on the computer?

   A $800 - 120 + 50 \div 2$ **C** $800 - (120 - 50) \div 2$

   B $[800 - (120 - 50) \div 2]$ **D** $[800 - (120 + 50)] \div 2$

15. **Number Sense** A printing error in a math book removed the brackets and parentheses from the original expression of $(7 \times 3.4) - [(2.8 \times 5) - (4.3 \times 2)] + 4^2$. Give the order of operations a student solving this problem would have used to evaluate the expression with the printing error, and find the value of the incorrect expression and the correct expression.

_____

_____

16. **Writing to Explain** How would you add parentheses and brackets to make this sentence true: $45 \div 2 \times 4.7 - 4.4 \times 6 = 54$

_____

Scientific Notation

Write each number in scientific notation.

1. 25,400,000

2. 0.0037

3. 918,000,000

_____

_____

_____

4. 0.0000021

5. 7,820,000,000

6. 0.00008134

_____

_____

_____

7. 6,000

8. 0.000000002

9. 48,020,000,000,000

_____

_____

_____

Write each number in standard form.

10. 3.2×10^4

11. 1.6×10^{-3}

12. 4.38×10^8

_____

_____

_____

13. 2.617×10^{-7}

14. 5.6×10^5

15. 2.915×10^{-10}

_____

_____

_____

Write the missing power of 10.

16. 34,800,000

$3.48 \times 10^{\square}$

17. 0.000903

$9.03 \times 10^{\square}$

18. 530,000,000,000

$5.3 \times 10^{\square}$

19. 0.0000000286

$2.86 \times 10^{\square}$

20. 8,750,000,000

$8.75 \times 10^{\square}$

21. 0.00000436

$4.36 \times 10^{\square}$

22. The U.S. Census Bureau estimates that in 2006, there were 9.7×10^{-1} males for every female. Write this number in standard form.

_____

23. In 2003, the population of the United States consumed 3,656,000,000,000 kilowatt hours of electricity. Write this number in scientific notation.

_____

24. A light wave with a length of 4.1×10^{-11} meters will appear violet to the human eye. Which shows that number in standard form?

A 0.0000000041

C 0.000000000041

B 0.00000000041

D 0.0000000000041

25. Writing to Explain In the number 8.3×10^{-8}, what is the value of 10^{-8}? How did you determine your answer?

_____

_____

Problem Solving:
Multiple-Step Problems

1. At a school concert, the orchestra plays 8 songs that are 4.25 min long and 3 songs that are twice as long as each of the others. How long is the concert?

_____

2. A shoe store sold 53 pairs of shoes on Monday and 35 pairs on Tuesday. On Wednesday, the store sold as many pairs of shoes as they sold on Monday and Tuesday combined. They sold half as many on Thursday as Wednesday. How many pairs of shoes did the shoe store sell Monday through Thursday?

_____

3. **Write a Problem** Use a real-life situation to create a problem in which there is a hidden question. Then identify the hidden question and the answer.

_____

_____

_____

_____

4. **Critical Thinking** Jackson is writing a report on California missions. He spent 2 hours researching missions on the Internet and three times as long writing the report. What is the hidden question if you want to find how many total hours Jackson spent on the report?

   A   How many hours did he spend researching and writing the report?

   B   How many hours did he spend researching the report?

   C   How much longer did it take to write the report than research it?

   D   How many hours did he spend writing the report?

5. **Writing to Explain** Explain how you can find the hidden questions in problem 2.

_____

_____

_____

_____

Properties of Equality

1. If $16 + 4 = 20$, does $16 + 4 - 4 = 20 - 4$? Why or why not?

_____

2. If $2d \div 4 = 5$, does $2d \div 4 + 6 = 5 + 4$? Why or why not?

_____

3. If $12 - 8 = 4$, does $(12 - 8) \div 2 = 4 \times 2$? Explain.

_____

4. If $7t = 70$, does $12 \times 7t = 12 \times 70$? Explain.

_____

5. **Critical Thinking** Emil and Jade have equal amounts of play money in two piles. Emil has $1 and a quarter in his pile. Jade has 5 quarters in her pile. If Emil gives Jade $1 and Jade gives Emil 4 quarters, will the two piles still be equal in value? Explain.

_____

_____

_____

6. Which equation shows the Multiplication Property of Equality if $n + 4 = 11$?

   A $(n + 4) \times 2 = 11$ **B** $(n + 4) \times 2 = 11 \div 2$

   C $(n + 4) \times 2 = 11 \times 4$ **D** $(n + 4) \times 2 = 11 \times 2$

7. **Writing to Explain** Bobbie wrote $y + 6 = 15$. Then she wrote $(y + 6) \div 3 = 15$. Explain why the second equation is not balanced and how to balance it.

_____

_____

_____

Solving Addition and Subtraction Equations

Explain how to get the variable alone in each equation.

1. $n + 10 = 100$
       $n + 10 - 10 = 100 - 10$

2. $x - 75 = 49$
       $x - 75 + \underline{\ \ } = 49 + \underline{\ \ }$

_____

_____

Solve each equation and check your answer.

3. $g - 8 = 25$

4. $25 + y = 42$

5. $r + 82 = 97$

_____

_____

_____

6. $30 = m - 18$

7. $150 = e + 42$

8. $a - 51 = 12$

_____

_____

_____

9. Jo loaned Al $15. She had $15 left. Solve the equation $15 = s - 15$ to find how much money Jo had before she made the loan.

  A $0

  B $15

  C $30

  D $60

10. Critical Thinking If $n + 10 = 40$, then what is the value of the expression $n - 25$?

  A 5

  B 25

  C 30

  D 50

11. Writing to Explain Explain how to solve the equation $35 + p = 92$. Then solve.

_____

Problem Solving: Draw a Picture and Write an Equation

Draw a picture and write an equation to solve each problem.

1. Mike has already driven 176 laps. The race is 250 laps long. How many more laps does he have to drive to finish the race?

_____

2. Antonio found 133 golf balls in the water. He picked up a total of 527 lost golf balls. How many golf balls did he find in the weeds and bushes?

_____

3. A lumber company plants 840 trees. If the company cuts down 560 trees, how many more trees did it plant than it cut down?

_____

4. Writing to Explain What operation would you use to solve this problem? Why?

> Erik wants to buy a new stereo for $359. He has $288 saved already. How much more will he have to save to buy the stereo?

_____

_____

5. Reasonableness Write an estimate that will show if 77 is a reasonable solution to the equation $14 + m = 91$.

_____

6. Juan brought 87 pounds of recyclables to the recycling center. He brought 54 pounds of glass, and the rest was plastic. Which equation could be used to find p, the number of pounds of plastic Juan recycled?

A $87 + p = 54$ **C** $p - 54 = 87$

B $54 + p = 87$ **D** $p + 87 = 54$

Solving Multiplication and Division Equations

For **1** through **3**, explain how to get the variable alone in each equation.

1. $r \times 7 = 42$
$r \times 7 \div 7 = 42 \div 7$

2. $m \div 6 = 12$
$m \div 6 \times \underline{\quad} = 12 \times \underline{\quad}$

3. $44 = 2k$

_____   _____   _____

For **4** through **9**, solve the equation. Check your answer.

4. $9n = 72$

5. $y \times 5 = 60$

6. $v \div 13 = 2$

_____   _____   _____

7. $w \div 7 = 15$

8. $216 = 36p$

9. $17 = t \div 3$

_____   _____   _____

10. Writing to Explain Tell how you would get the variable m alone on one side of the equation $15m = 45$.

_____

_____

11. Write a Problem Write a problem that can be solved with the equation $r \div 6 = 14$.

_____

_____

12. Number Sense Which equation can you use to solve this problem?

There are 12 muffins in a package. Will bought 84 muffins. How many packages did he buy?

A $12 \times p = 84$

B $84 \times 12 = p$

C $12 \div p = 84$

D $84 = 12 + p$

Problem Solving: Draw a Picture and Write an Equation

Draw a picture and write an equation to solve each problem.

1. Mr. Conover bought 6 boxes of pastels for his art class. He paid $4.50 for each box. What was the total cost of the boxes?

   _____

2. A company charters boats for whale watching. The company chartered 13 boats. There were a total of 325 passengers on the boats. What was the average number of passengers per boat?

   _____

3. A store sells 5-gallon bottles of water for $8. The store made $288 on Monday selling the water. How many bottles were sold?

   _____

4. A sign at a recycling center states that 118 pounds of recycled newspapers saves one tree. How many pounds of newspapers will save 3 trees?

   _____

5. **Algebra** Students mailed invitations to a play to 414 parents. Each student mailed 18 invitations. If s equals the number of students who mailed invitations, which equation best shows the number of invitations that were mailed?

   A $s + 18 = 414$ **C** $18 \div s = 414$

   B $s \div 18 = 414$ **D** $18s = 414$

Factors, Multiples, and Divisibility

Tell whether each number is divisible by 2, 3, 4, 5, 6, 9, or 10.

1. 27 _____

2. 86 _____

3. 348 _____

4. 954 _____

Tell whether each number is a multiple of the second.

5. 78; 2 _____

6. 535; 3 _____

7. Number Sense Name 3 numbers that are factors of both 15 and 30.

_____

The sixth graders at Washington Middle School researched the history of their city. The students then gave a presentation to the other students at the school.

8. If there were 64 sixth graders, list all of the ways they could have been divided equally into groups of 10 or fewer students.

_____

_____

9. Only 60 sixth graders were present. Of the 60, 14 were needed to run the light and sound equipment during the presentation. How could the remaining students be divided into equal groups of 6 or fewer students to read the presentation?

_____

10. The 60 students were transported in vans to the high school to share their presentation. If the vans carry a maximum of 7 students each, what was the minimum number of vans required to carry the students to the high school?

_____

11. Which of the following numbers is divisible by both 9 and 4?

A 24,815 **B** 18,324 **C** 9,140 **D** 9,126

12. Writing in Math If a number is divisible by both 2 and 6, is it always divisible by 12? Use examples in your answer.

_____

Prime Factorization

For **1** through **10** if the number is prime, write *prime.* If the number is composite, write the prime factorization.

1. 24 _____

2. 43 _____

3. 51 _____

4. 66 _____

5. 61 _____

6. 96 _____

7. 144 _____

8. 243 _____

9. 270 _____

10. 124 _____

11. Writing to Explain Find the first ten prime numbers. Tell how you do it.

_____

_____

12. Reasoning How many even prime numbers are there?

A 0

B 1

C 2

D 3

13. Critical Thinking Which answer completes the sentence below?

The number 1 is _____.

A prime.

B composite.

C neither prime nor composite.

D both prime and composite.

Name _____

Greatest Common Factor

Find the GCF for each set of numbers.

1. 12, 48 _____   **2.** 20, 24 _____   **3.** 21, 84 _____

4. 24, 100 _____   **5.** 18, 130 _____   **6.** 200, 205 _____

7. Number Sense Name three pairs of numbers
that have 5 as their greatest common factor.
Use each number only once in your answer.

_____

8. The bake-sale committee divided each type of item
evenly onto plates, so that every plate contained
only one type of item and every plate had exactly the
same number of items with no leftovers. What is the
maximum number of items that could have been
placed on each plate?

Bake Sale Donations	
Muffins	96
Bread sticks	48
Rolls	84

_____

9. Using this system, how many plates of rolls could the
bake-sale committee make? _____

10. Using this system, how many plates of muffins could
the bake-sale committee make? _____

11. Which of the following pairs of numbers is correctly listed with its
greatest common factor?

    A 20, 24; GCF: 4

    B 50, 100; GCF: 25

    C 4, 6; GCF: 24

    D 15, 20; GCF: 10

12. Writing to Explain Explain one method of finding the greatest
common factor of 48 and 84.

_____

_____

_____

Name _____

Understanding Fractions

Write the fraction that represents the shaded portion.

1.

_____

2.

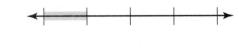

_____

3.

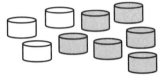

_____

4.

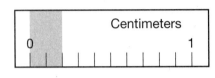

_____

Draw models of fractions.

5. Draw a set to represent $\frac{4}{10}$.

6. Draw a number line to represent $\frac{1}{6}$.

7. Write a Problem Write a fraction problem that can be solved using this model.

_____

8. Writing to Explain Sharon drew this drawing to show $\frac{3}{5}$. Is her drawing correct? Explain why or why not.

_____

9. Estimation Which is the best estimate of how full the cup is?

A $\frac{3}{4}$ full

B $\frac{1}{2}$ full

C $\frac{1}{3}$ full

D $\frac{1}{8}$ full

Equivalent Fractions

Find two fractions equivalent to each fraction.

1. $\frac{5}{6}$ _____   **2.** $\frac{15}{30}$ _____   **3.** $\frac{45}{60}$ _____

4. $\frac{7}{8}$ _____   **5.** $\frac{20}{8}$ _____   **6.** $\frac{16}{32}$ _____

7. $\frac{36}{60}$ _____   **8.** $\frac{32}{96}$ _____   **9.** $\frac{2}{3}$ _____

10. **Number Sense** Are the fractions $\frac{1}{5}$, $\frac{5}{5}$, and $\frac{5}{1}$ equivalent? Explain.

_____

11. The United States currently has 50 states. What fraction of the states had become a part of the United States by 1795? Write your answer as two equivalent fractions.

Number of States in the United States

Year	Number of States
1795	15
1848	30
1900	45
1915	48
1960	50

_____

12. In what year was the total number of states in the United States $\frac{3}{5}$ the number it was in 1960?

_____

13. The United States currently has 50 states. Write two fractions that describe the number of states that had become part of the United States in 1915?

_____

14. Which of the following pairs of fractions are equivalent?

A $\frac{1}{10}$, $\frac{3}{33}$

B $\frac{9}{5}$, $\frac{5}{9}$

C $\frac{5}{45}$, $\frac{1}{9}$

D $\frac{6}{8}$, $\frac{34}{48}$

15. **Writing to Explain** In what situation can you use only multiplication to find equivalent fractions to a given fraction? Give an example.

_____

_____

Fractions in Simplest Form

Write each fraction in simplest form.

1. $\frac{8}{16}$ _____

2. $\frac{15}{20}$ _____

3. $\frac{10}{12}$ _____

4. $\frac{20}{35}$ _____

5. $\frac{16}{48}$ _____

6. $\frac{45}{100}$ _____

7. $\frac{60}{96}$ _____

8. $\frac{72}{75}$ _____

9. $\frac{32}{36}$ _____

10. $\frac{8}{28}$ _____

11. $\frac{21}{56}$ _____

12. $\frac{63}{81}$ _____

13. **Number Sense** How can you check to see if a fraction is written in simplest form?

_____

_____

14. **Writing to Explain** What is the GCF and how is it used to find the simplest form of a fraction?

_____

_____

_____

Find the GCF of the numerator and denominator of the fraction.

15. $\frac{8}{26}$ _____

16. $\frac{30}{75}$ _____

17. $\frac{48}{72}$ _____

Use the GCF to write each fraction in simplest form.

18. $\frac{12}{16}$ _____

19. $\frac{12}{20}$ _____

20. $\frac{30}{36}$ _____

21. $\frac{35}{56}$ _____

22. $\frac{28}{63}$ _____

23. $\frac{42}{72}$ _____

24. What is the simplest form of the fraction $\frac{81}{108}$?

    A $\frac{28}{36}$

    B $\frac{3}{4}$

    C $\frac{2}{3}$

    D $\frac{4}{5}$

Problem Solving: Make and Test Conjectures

Test these conjectures. Give three examples. Explain if the conjecture is *reasonable* or *not reasonable*.

1. If a number is divisible by 4, it is always an even number.

   _____

2. The product of two integers is always positive.

   _____

3. If a number has a 9 in the ones place, it is always divisible by 3.

   _____

4. The least common denominator of two fractions is always greater than the denominators of the fractions.

   _____

5. Write a conjecture about the product of two odd numbers. Then test your conjecture.

   _____

   _____

6. Write a conjecture about the difference of two negative integers. Then test your conjecture.

   _____

   _____

7. **Reasoning** How is testing a conjecture like finding a statement true or false? How is it different?

   _____

   _____

   _____

Fractions and Division

Write a division expression for each fraction.

1. $\frac{4}{10}$ _____

2. $\frac{1}{6}$ _____

3. $\frac{2}{7}$ _____

4. $\frac{3}{8}$ _____

5. $\frac{5}{12}$ _____

6. $\frac{3}{17}$ _____

7. $\frac{7}{9}$ _____

8. $\frac{18}{25}$ _____

9. $\frac{99}{100}$ _____

Write each division expression as a fraction.

10. $7 \div 12$ _____

11. $2 \div 5$ _____

12. $8 \div 11$ _____

13. $1 \div 8$ _____

14. $7 \div 10$ _____

15. $6 \div 13$ _____

16. $5 \div 9$ _____

17. $11 \div 21$ _____

18. $13 \div 100$ _____

19. Zane was telling his mother that he learned about rational numbers in school. Which is the definition of a rational number?

   A Any number that can be shown as the quotient of two integers

   B Any number that can be shown as the product of two integers

   C Any number that can be written as an integer

   D Any integer that can be written as a decimal

20. Tanisha used the division expression $2 \div 5$ to equally divide two same-size pizzas among five people. Which fraction represents each person's share of the pizza?

   A $\frac{5}{2}$

   B $\frac{2}{5}$

   C $\frac{2}{7}$

   D $\frac{5}{7}$

21. **Writing to Explain** Can the division expression $-4 \div 15$ be shown as a fraction? If yes, write the fraction. Explain why or why not.

   _____

   _____

Fractions and Decimals

Write a decimal and a fraction in simplest form for each shaded portion.

1.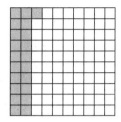

_____

2.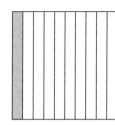

_____

Write each decimal as a fraction in simplest form.

3. 0.15 _____   **4.** 0.31 _____   **5.** 0.82 _____

6. 0.27 _____   **7.** 0.375 _____   **8.** 0.920 _____

Convert each fraction to a decimal.

9. $\frac{56}{100}$ _____   **10.** $\frac{90}{200}$ _____   **11.** $\frac{9}{25}$ _____

12. $\frac{8}{50}$ _____   **13.** $\frac{57}{60}$ _____   **14.** $\frac{7}{8}$ _____

15. Draw a Picture Show $\frac{46}{200}$ on the hundredths grid. Then write the fraction as a decimal.

_____

16. About $\frac{2}{5}$ of the students in the after school program have a cell phone. Which decimal is equivalent to $\frac{2}{5}$?

A   0.2

B   0.25

C   0.4

D   0.5

17. Writing to Explain Solve the problem. Then explain how you found the answer. In Tori's favorite class, $\frac{12}{25}$ of the students are girls. Write a decimal that represents the number of boys in the class.

_____

_____

Name _____

Improper Fractions and Mixed Numbers

1. Draw a picture to show $\frac{9}{7}$.

2. Draw a picture to show $3\frac{4}{5}$.

Write each improper fraction as a whole number or mixed number in simplest form.

3. $\frac{25}{5}$ _____

4. $\frac{47}{9}$ _____

5. $\frac{52}{7}$ _____

Write each mixed number as an improper fraction.

6. $4\frac{4}{5}$ _____

7. $13\frac{3}{4}$ _____

8. $9\frac{5}{8}$ _____

9. **Reasoning** Write 8 as an improper fraction with a denominator of 4.

_____

Which letter on the number line corresponds to each number?

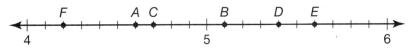

10. $5\frac{2}{5}$ _____

11. $4\frac{7}{10}$ _____

12. $\frac{23}{5}$ _____

13. Which number does the picture show?

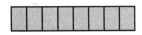 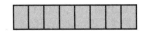 

    A $\frac{12}{8}$

    B $2\frac{1}{8}$

    C $2\frac{1}{4}$

    D $\frac{20}{8}$

14. **Writing to Explain** Can you express $\frac{9}{9}$ as a mixed number? Why or why not?

_____

_____

40

Decimal Forms of Fractions and Mixed Numbers

Write each fraction or mixed number as a decimal.

1. $\frac{33}{100}$ _____

2. $\frac{2}{5}$ _____

3. $\frac{1}{6}$ _____

4. $1\frac{3}{16}$ _____

5. $4\frac{7}{9}$ _____

6. $6\frac{5}{11}$ _____

Write each decimal as a fraction or a mixed number in simplest form.

7. 0.08 _____

8. 0.24 _____

9. 0.325 _____

10. 4.75 _____

11. 1.06 _____

12. 5.15 _____

13. The label on a cosmetic bottle says 0.04 oz. What is the fraction equivalent for this amount? _____

14. The scale at a deli counter shows 2.54 lb. What is the mixed number equivalent for the number shown? _____

15. **Reasoning** What is a situation in which you would use fractions to express a number less than one? What is a situation in which decimals seem to work better?

_____

_____

16. Which decimal is equivalent to $4\frac{4}{5}$?

   A 4.4

   B 4.45

   C $4.\overline{5}$

   D 4.8

17. **Writing to Explain** How do you know where to place the bar when a decimal is a repeating decimal?

_____

_____

Problem Solving: Draw a Picture

1. A community swimming pool places buoys every 1.5 feet across the pool to mark off swimming areas. Use your ruler and the number line to show where each buoy is placed.

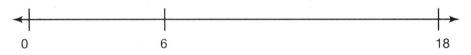

feet

2. A trail is marked every 0.6 mile. Use the number line below to show the start of the trail if the trail is 5.4 miles long.

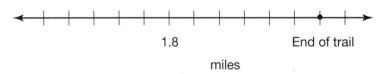

miles

3. A conveyer belt at a factory moves parts from station to station. The stations are 0.75 feet apart. Draw and label a number line that shows stops at 0.75, 2.25, and 4.5 feet.

4. Kayla drew the number line to show the distance between Fontana and Rialto. If Fontana is 0, what is the label at Rialto?

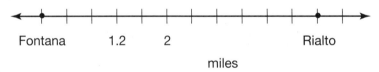

miles

A 4.2

B 4.4

C 4.8

D 5.2

5. **Writing to Explain** Maggie is planting bushes every 1.5 feet along the side of a fence. The fence is 22.5 feet long. Explain how Maggie can draw a picture to show where each bush is planted.

_____

_____

Adding and Subtracting: Like Denominators

Find each sum or difference. Use a number line. Simplify your answers.

1. $\frac{7}{8} - \frac{3}{8}$ _____

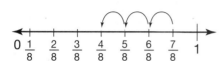

$0 \; \frac{1}{8} \; \frac{2}{8} \; \frac{3}{8} \; \frac{4}{8} \; \frac{5}{8} \; \frac{6}{8} \; \frac{7}{8} \; 1$

2. $\frac{3}{5} + \frac{4}{5}$ _____

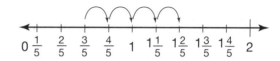

$0 \; \frac{1}{5} \; \frac{2}{5} \; \frac{3}{5} \; \frac{4}{5} \; 1 \; 1\frac{1}{5} \; 1\frac{2}{5} \; 1\frac{3}{5} \; 1\frac{4}{5} \; 2$

Find each sum or difference. Simplify your answers.

3. $\frac{6}{7} + \frac{1}{7}$ _____

4. $\frac{9}{10} - \frac{4}{10}$ _____

5. $\frac{8}{15} - \frac{5}{15}$ _____

6. $\frac{1}{11} + \frac{3}{11} + \frac{4}{11}$ _____

7. $\frac{1}{6} + \frac{2}{6} + \frac{5}{6}$ _____

8. $\frac{2}{20} + \frac{5}{20} + \frac{7}{20}$ _____

Evaluate **9** through **11** for $x = \frac{2}{9}$.

9. $\frac{8}{9} + x$ _____

10. $\frac{5}{9} - x$ _____

11. $\left(\frac{7}{9} - x\right) + \frac{1}{9}$ _____

12. Use the table to answer the questions.

   a. What is the total amount of seafood in the soup?

   _____

   b. How much more shrimp than cod is in the soup?

   _____

Seafood for Soup	
Cod	$\frac{5}{8}$ lb
Scallops	$\frac{2}{8}$ lb
Shrimp	$\frac{7}{8}$ lb

13. Critical Thinking Max has 12 pairs of socks. Of them, 6 pairs are blue, 3 pairs are brown, and 2 pairs are white. Max wants to know what fraction of the socks are blue or brown. How can he find the numerator?

   A Add 6 + 3 + 2.

   B Add 6 + 3.

   C Subtract 11 from 12.

   D Subtract 9 from 12.

14. Writing to Explain Explain how you can add two fractions with denominators of 10 and end up with a sum whose denominator is 5.

_____

_____

Name _____

Least Common Multiple

Find the LCM of each set of numbers.

1. 15, 20 _____   **2.** 4, 50 _____   **3.** 8, 12 _____

4. 14, 42 _____   **5.** 21, 30 _____   **6.** 3, 7, 10 _____

7. 6, 7, 8 _____   **8.** 16, 20 _____   **9.** 12, 16 _____

10. At what times of the day between 10:00 A.M. and 5:00 P.M. do the chemistry presentation and the recycling presentation start at the same time?

_____

_____

Science Museum
— Show Schedule —
Chemistry — Every 30 minutes
Electricity — Every 20 minutes
Recycling — Every 40 minutes
Fossils — Every 45 minutes
The first showing for all shows is at 10:00 A.M.

11. The museum does shows in schools every Monday and shows in public libraries every fifth day (on both weekdays and weekends). If the museum did both a school show and a library show on Monday, how many days will it be until it does both shows on the same day again?

_____

12. Which of the following pairs of numbers is correctly listed with its LCM?

　A 5, 15; LCM: 30

　B 20, 30; LCM: 60

　C 24, 36; LCM: 12

　D 7, 9; LCM: 21

13. Writing to Explain What method would you use to find the LCM of a group of four numbers? Explain and give an example.

_____

_____

_____

_____

_____

Adding and Subtracting: Unlike Denominators

Find each sum or difference. Simplify your answer.

1. $\frac{5}{6} + \frac{4}{12} =$ _____

2. $\frac{4}{5} - \frac{1}{10} =$ _____

3. $\frac{5}{12} + \frac{2}{3} =$ _____

4. $\frac{9}{20} + \frac{3}{5} =$ _____

5. $\frac{6}{16} - \frac{1}{4} =$ _____

6. $\frac{19}{21} - \frac{2}{7} =$ _____

7. $\frac{2}{5} + \frac{5}{20} =$ _____

8. $\frac{8}{9} - \frac{5}{12} =$ _____

9. $\frac{7}{8} + \frac{11}{24} - \frac{5}{6} =$ _____

10. Number Sense Is $\frac{7}{8}$ or $\frac{11}{10}$ closer to 1? How did you decide?

_____

_____

Emma has a small garden. Emma's garden is $\frac{1}{5}$ beans, $\frac{1}{8}$ peas, and $\frac{1}{2}$ corn. The rest is planted with flowers.

11. What fraction of Emma's garden is planted with vegetables?

_____

_____

12. Are there more flowers or peas in Emma's garden?

_____

_____

13. To solve the subtraction sentence $\frac{17}{10} - \frac{2}{5} = ?$, which common denominator is the best choice?

    A 10

    B 15

    C 20

    D 50

14. Writing to Explain To find the sum of $\frac{4}{9}$ and $\frac{7}{12}$, Mario rewrites the fractions as $\frac{8}{36}$ and $\frac{21}{36}$. His answer is $\frac{29}{36}$. Is Mario right? If not, show his error and correct it.

_____

_____

Name _____

Practice

7-4

Estimating Sums and Differences of Mixed Numbers

Round to the nearest whole number.

1. $3\frac{4}{9}$ _____

2. $5\frac{6}{7}$ _____

3. $2\frac{2}{5}$ _____

4. $11\frac{12}{15}$ _____

Estimate each sum or difference.

5. $2\frac{1}{4} + 3\frac{5}{6}$ _____

6. $5\frac{6}{9} - 1\frac{3}{4}$ _____

7. $8\frac{5}{13} + 5\frac{3}{5}$ _____

8. $11 - 6\frac{3}{7} + 2\frac{2}{5}$ _____

Rodrigo and Mel are competing in a track meet. The table at the right shows the results of their events.

9. Rodrigo claims his best jump was about 1 ft longer than Mel's best jump. Is he correct?

_____

_____

Participant	Event	Results/Distance
Rodrigo	Long jump	**1.** $6\frac{3}{8}$ ft **2.** $5\frac{5}{6}$ ft
	Softball throw	$62\frac{1}{5}$ ft
Mel	Long jump	**1.** $4\frac{7}{10}$ ft **2.** $4\frac{3}{4}$ ft
	Softball throw	$71\frac{7}{8}$ ft

10. Use the table above. If the school record for the softball throw is 78 ft, about how much farther must Rodrigo throw the ball to match the record?

A 15 ft   **B** 16 ft   **C** 18 ft   **D** 20 ft

11. **Writing to Explain** Consider the sum of $\frac{3}{5} + \frac{3}{4}$. Round each fraction and estimate the sum. Add the two fractions using a common denominator and then round the result. Which estimate is closest to the actual answer?

_____

_____

_____

_____

46

Adding Mixed Numbers

Find each sum. Simplify your answer.

1. $5 + 3\frac{1}{6} =$ _____

2. $4\frac{4}{5} + 8\frac{1}{10} =$ _____

3. $1\frac{5}{8} + \frac{15}{16} =$ _____

4. $6\frac{2}{3} + \frac{5}{4} =$ _____

5. $2\frac{7}{8} + 4 =$ _____

6. $7\frac{6}{10} + 1\frac{9}{20} =$ _____

7. $\frac{7}{8} + 3\frac{3}{5} + 2 =$ _____

8. $9 + 3\frac{2}{3} + \frac{5}{6} =$ _____

9. **Number Sense** Give an example of two mixed numbers whose sum is a whole number.

_____

_____

_____

10. An ostrich egg is $6\frac{4}{5}$ in. long. A California condor's egg is $4\frac{3}{10}$ in. long, and an albatross egg is $5\frac{7}{10}$ in. long. If the three eggs are placed end to end, what is the total length in inches? _____

11. Shanda can travel 10 mi on her electric scooter before she has to recharge the batteries. If it is $4\frac{5}{8}$ mi to the library and $5\frac{2}{5}$ mi to her friend's house, can she make both trips before she needs to recharge the batteries?

_____

_____

12. Which is the fractional portion of the solution to $5\frac{3}{8} + 2\frac{3}{12}$?

    A $\frac{6}{12}$

    B $\frac{5}{8}$

    C $\frac{6}{8}$

    D $\frac{15}{8}$

13. **Writing to Explain** Explain the steps to adding mixed numbers. What must you do first?

_____

_____

Subtracting Mixed Numbers

Find each difference. Simplify if possible.

1. $2\frac{3}{5} - 1\frac{1}{5} =$ _____

2. $1\frac{4}{9} - \frac{8}{9} =$ _____

3. $5\frac{5}{8} - 1\frac{9}{16} =$ _____

4. $12 - 4\frac{5}{6} =$ _____

5. $6\frac{15}{16} - 4 =$ _____

6. $3\frac{7}{12} - 2\frac{3}{4} =$ _____

7. $9 - 7\frac{5}{8} =$ _____

8. $15\frac{1}{6} - 8\frac{2}{3} =$ _____

9. $6\frac{8}{9} - 1\frac{2}{3} =$ _____

10. $2\frac{3}{7} - 1\frac{5}{14} =$ _____

11. In which of the exercises above do you have to rename the first mixed number to show more fractional parts before subtracting?

_____

The table at the right shows the lengths of various carpentry nails.

12. How much longer is a 30d nail than a 5d nail?

_____

13. How much longer is a 12d nail than a 9d nail?

Carpentry Nails

Size	Length (inches)
5d	$1\frac{3}{4}$
9d	$2\frac{3}{4}$
12d	$3\frac{1}{4}$
30d	$4\frac{1}{2}$

_____

14. To subtract $4\frac{5}{6}$ from $10\frac{1}{3}$, which of the following must the mixed number $10\frac{1}{3}$ first be renamed as?

A $9\frac{2}{3}$

B $9\frac{4}{6}$

C $9\frac{8}{6}$

D $10\frac{2}{6}$

15. Writing to Explain Jack says that once you have a common denominator you are ready to subtract two mixed numbers. What other step might be necessary before you can subtract? Give an example.

_____

_____

_____

Problem Solving:
Make a Table

Make tables to solve. Write each answer in a complete sentence.

1. A train has 3 engines, 52 boxcars, and 1 caboose. At every stop, it picks up 8 more boxcars. How many total cars (engines, cars, and cabooses) will the train have after 5 stops?

_____

2. Eileen likes to keep scrapbooks. She already has 4 scrapbooks filled with 40 pages each. If she fills 5 pages every month, how many months will it take her to fill up 2 more 40-page scrapbooks?

_____

3. Phil's Garage charges $50 for towing and $40 per hour to fix a car. Cliff's Cars charges $60 for towing and $38 per hour to fix a car. After how many hours of working on a car will the cost of towing and fixing a car be the same at the two repair shops?

_____

4. Dominic got a new video game. The first time he played the game he scored 80 points. After that, each time he played he increased his score by 60 points. How many times will he have to play before he scores 500 points?

_____

5. A scientist is studying certain germs. She places 3 germs in a special solution that will help the germs grow. The number of germs doubles every hour. How many germs will there be after 8 hours?

 A 24 **B** 384 **C** 768 **D** 786

6. **Writing to Explain** Ed saved $50 one week. For the next 6 weeks, he saved $25 more than he saved the week before. How much did he save in all? One student solved this problem using the expression $50 + 6($25) = $200. What error was made? What is the correct answer?

_____

_____

_____

Multiplying a Fraction and a Whole Number

Find each product.

1. $\frac{3}{4} \times 16 =$ _____

2. $\frac{5}{6} \times 30 =$ _____

3. $42 \times \frac{5}{6} =$ _____

4. $\frac{1}{8}$ of $72 =$ _____

5. $900 \times \frac{2}{3} =$ _____

6. $\frac{13}{20}$ of $100 =$ _____

7. **Reasoning** Without multiplying, tell which is greater, $\frac{5}{6}$ of 81 or $\frac{9}{10}$ of 81. Explain.

_____

Driving Distances

Departure City	Destination City	Distance
Pittsfield, Massachusetts	Providence, Rhode Island	132 mi
Reno, Nevada	Wendover, Utah	400 mi

8. Mike drove $\frac{1}{3}$ of the distance between Pittsfield, Massachusetts, and Providence, Rhode Island. How far did he drive?

_____

9. Bimal drove $\frac{3}{5}$ of the distance between Reno, Nevada, and Wendover, Utah. How far did he drive?

_____

10. **Estimation** How many more miles does Bimal have to drive to get to Wendover, Utah?

_____

11. There are 25 students in Mr. Fitch's sixth-grade class. If $\frac{3}{5}$ of the students are girls, how many girls are in Mr. Fitch's class?

A 5 girls   **B** 10 girls   **C** 15 girls   **D** 20 girls

12. **Writing to Explain** Explain how you would find the product of 36 and $\frac{2}{3}$.

_____

_____

_____

Estimating Products

Estimate each product.

1. $4\frac{5}{8} \times \frac{1}{3} =$ _____

2. $3 \times 2\frac{1}{5} =$ _____

3. $\frac{6}{10} \times 5\frac{3}{4} =$ _____

4. $2\frac{7}{9} \times 4\frac{2}{5} =$ _____

5. $6\frac{1}{2} \times 2\frac{1}{3} =$ _____

6. $\frac{7}{8} \times 2\frac{3}{8} =$ _____

7. $38 \times \frac{3}{8} =$ _____

8. $\frac{1}{4} \times 17 =$ _____

9. $\frac{3}{5} \times 51 =$ _____

10. $7\frac{4}{9} \times 5\frac{6}{7} =$ _____

11. $\frac{12}{25} \times 8 =$ _____

12. $11 \times \frac{1}{2} =$ _____

13. $\frac{8}{9} \times 6\frac{4}{10} =$ _____

14. $7\frac{1}{7} \times 2\frac{2}{3} =$ _____

15. $\frac{5}{} \times 13 =$ _____

16. Show three ways to estimate $\frac{3}{5} \times 5\frac{3}{4}$. Identify each method you use.

_____

_____

17. **Explain It** Mr. Simpson lives $11\frac{3}{10}$ miles from his office. He estimates that he commutes $11 \times 2 \times 5$, or 110 miles each week. Is his estimate an overestimate or an underestimate? Explain.

_____

_____

18. Which benchmark fraction could you use to estimate the product of $38 \times \frac{7}{12}$? _____

19. **Geometry** Which is the best estimate for the area of a square with sides equal to $3\frac{1}{5}$ inches?

A 3 sq in.
B 6 sq in.
C 9 sq in.
D 16 sq in.

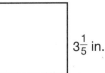

$3\frac{1}{5}$ in.

20. Joyce and Marianne have money jars. Joyce has 54 dimes in her jar. Marianne has $\frac{9}{10}$ as many dimes as Joyce. Estimate the number of dimes that Marianne has in her jar.

A 60 dimes
B 45 dimes
C 6 dimes
D 5 dimes

Multiplying Fractions

Write an equation for each picture.

1.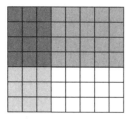

2.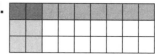

_____

_____

Find each product. Simplify if possible.

3. $\frac{7}{10} \times \frac{13}{14} =$ _____

4. $\frac{4}{5} \times \frac{7}{8} =$ _____

5. $\frac{3}{7} \times \frac{4}{9} =$ _____

6. $\frac{3}{4} \times 16 =$ _____

7. $\frac{2}{5} \times \frac{3}{10} =$ _____

8. $\frac{5}{6} \times 42 =$ _____

9. $\frac{3}{5} \times \frac{17}{21} =$ _____

10. $\frac{1}{8} \times 72 =$ _____

11. $\frac{15}{9} \times \frac{24}{25} =$ _____

12. $\frac{13}{20} \times 100 =$ _____

13. $\frac{3}{8} \times \frac{4}{9} =$ _____

14. $\frac{1}{2} \times \frac{13}{16} =$ _____

Pamela spent $\frac{2}{3}$ of an hour doing homework. She solved math problems for $\frac{2}{5}$ of that time and read her science book for $\frac{3}{5}$ of that time. What fraction of one hour did Pamela spend

15. solving math problems? _____

16. reading her science book? _____

17. Of the students in Mr. Moore's room, $\frac{7}{13}$ live within a mile of school. Of those students, $\frac{4}{7}$ live within half a mile of school. What fraction of all students in Mr. Moore's class live within half a mile of school?

    A $\frac{3}{13}$

    B $\frac{4}{13}$

    C $\frac{3}{15}$

    D $\frac{4}{15}$

18. Writing to Explain Without multiplying, tell which is greater: $\frac{55}{6} \times 81$ or $\frac{9}{10} \times 81$. Explain.

_____

_____

Multiplying Mixed Numbers

Find each product. Simplify if possible.

1. $3\frac{1}{2} \times 1\frac{2}{3}$ _____

2. $1\frac{1}{8} \times 2\frac{1}{3}$ _____

3. $7 \times 1\frac{1}{4}$ _____

4. $2\frac{1}{6} \times 1\frac{1}{5}$ _____

5. $3\frac{1}{6} \times 18$ _____

6. $1\frac{1}{8} \times 2\frac{1}{2}$ _____

7. $1\frac{2}{3} \times 2\frac{1}{4}$ _____

8. $10 \times 1\frac{1}{3}$ _____

9. $2\frac{4}{5} \times 3\frac{1}{3}$ _____

Evaluate each expression for $S = 1\frac{4}{5}$.

10. $2\frac{1}{3}S$ _____

11. $3\frac{3}{4}S$ _____

12. $5\frac{1}{6}S$ _____

Use the table to answer the questions.

13. If Berkeley receives $1\frac{1}{4}$ times its average January rainfall, how much rain will it receive?

_____

Average Rainfall in Berkeley, California	
January	$3\frac{7}{10}$ in.
April	$1\frac{4}{5}$ in.
October	$1\frac{1}{2}$ in.

14. How much rain will Berkeley receive if it is $2\frac{1}{3}$ times the October average?

_____

15. Which month has about twice the rainfall as April?

_____

16. Jessie stacked photographs of 6 zoo animals on top of each other to create a display. Each photo is $14\frac{1}{4}$ in. high. How high is the display?

   A $84\frac{2}{3}$ in.

   B $85\frac{1}{2}$ in.

   C $86\frac{3}{4}$ in.

   D 87 in.

17. Writing to Explain Explain how you would find $2 \times 2\frac{1}{3}$ using the Distributive Property.

_____

_____

Problem Solving: Multiple-Step Problems

Write and answer the hidden question(s) in each problem. Then solve the problem.

1. Tiwa spent $1\frac{1}{2}$ hours setting up her computer. It took her 3 times as long to install the software. How long did it take Tiwa to set up the computer and install software?

   Hidden question(s):_____

   Solution:_____

2. Lon bought 40 ounces of sliced ham. He used $\frac{3}{4}$ of the ham to make sandwiches for his friends and $\frac{1}{5}$ of the ham in an omelet. How many ounces of ham were left?

   Hidden question(s):_____

   Solution:_____

3. Lionel cut off $\frac{1}{6}$ of a 48-inch piece of rope. Marsha cut off $\frac{1}{4}$ of a 36-inch piece of rope. They compared their cut pieces. Whose piece is longer? How much longer?

   Hidden question(s):_____

   Solution:_____

4. Melanie bought 3 CDs. The country music CD cost $15. The rock music CD cost $\frac{2}{3}$ as much as the country music CD. The platinum edition CD cost twice as much as the rock CD. What was the cost of the three CDs?

   Hidden question(s):_____

   Solution:_____

5. **Writing to Explain** Choose one of the problems above. Explain how you determined the hidden question and why it was necessary to answer that question in order to solve the problem.

   _____

   _____

   _____

Understanding Division of Fractions

Solve each division sentence using the models provided.

1. $3 \div \frac{1}{3} =$ _____

0 1 2 3

2. $\frac{1}{4} \div 6 =$ _____

$\frac{1}{4}$

3. $\frac{5}{6} \div \frac{1}{6} =$ _____

0 $\frac{1}{6}$ $\frac{2}{6}$ $\frac{3}{6}$ $\frac{4}{6}$ $\frac{5}{6}$

Find each quotient. Simplify if possible.

4. $8 \div \frac{1}{4} =$ _____

5. $\frac{1}{7} \div 4 =$ _____

6. $5 \div \frac{1}{2} =$ _____

7. $\frac{7}{8} \div \frac{1}{8} =$ _____

8. $\frac{11}{12} \div \frac{1}{12} =$ _____

9. $\frac{1}{12} \div 3 =$ _____

10. $6 \div \frac{2}{3} =$ _____

11. $7 \div \frac{1}{3} =$ _____

12. $\frac{15}{16} \div \frac{1}{16} =$ _____

13. Draw a Picture Olivia has a piece of ribbon $\frac{1}{2}$ yard long. If she cuts it into 6 equal pieces, what will be the length of each piece, in yards?

_____

14. Geometry A regular polygon has a perimeter of 12 units. If each side measures $\frac{3}{4}$ unit, how many sides does the polygon have?

_____

15. Which division expression is shown by this model?

1 2 3 4 5 6 7 8 9

0                                    $\frac{9}{10}$

A $\frac{9}{10} \div \frac{1}{10}$ **B** $1 \div \frac{1}{10}$ **C** $\frac{9}{10} \div 1$ **D** $10 \div \frac{9}{10}$

16. Writing to Explain When you divide a whole number by a fraction less than 1, will the quotient be greater than or less than the whole number? Explain, and give an example.

_____

_____

_____

Dividing a Whole Number by a Fraction

Find the reciprocal of each fraction or whole number.

1. $\frac{5}{9}$ _____

2. 8 _____

3. $\frac{7}{3}$ _____

Find each quotient. Simplify if possible.

4. $8 \div \frac{2}{5} =$ _____

5. $4 \div \frac{1}{6} =$ _____

6. $18 \div \frac{3}{8} =$ _____

7. $12 \div \frac{1}{2} =$ _____

8. $42 \div \frac{7}{9} =$ _____

9. $10 \div \frac{5}{6} =$ _____

10. $20 \div \frac{3}{4} =$ _____

11. $22 \div \frac{5}{6} =$ _____

12. $7 \div \frac{2}{3} =$ _____

13. $9 \div \frac{1}{8} =$ _____

14. $15 \div \frac{1}{3} =$ _____

15. $6 \div \frac{1}{5} =$ _____

16. Writing to Explain Will the quotient of $5 \div \frac{7}{8}$ be greater than or less than 5? Explain.

_____

17. Reasoning How many times will you need to fill a $\frac{1}{2}$ cup measuring cup to measure 4 cups of flour?

_____

18. Geometry The distance around a circular flower bed is 36 feet. Jasper wants to put stakes every 8 inches ($\frac{2}{3}$ of a foot) around the bed. How many stakes does he need?

_____

19. Algebra Which expression is equal to $9 \times \frac{3}{2}$?

 A $2 \div \frac{3}{9}$

 B $3 \div \frac{9}{2}$

 C $9 \div \frac{2}{3}$

 D $9 \div \frac{3}{2}$

Dividing Fractions

Find each quotient. Simplify if possible.

1. $\frac{1}{3} \div \frac{5}{6} = $ _____

2. $\frac{3}{8} \div \frac{1}{2} = $ _____

3. $\frac{7}{8} \div \frac{7}{12} = $ _____

4. $\frac{5}{9} \div 5 = $ _____

5. $\frac{6}{7} \div \frac{3}{4} = $ _____

6. $\frac{2}{3} \div \frac{3}{4} = $ _____

7. $\frac{1}{2} \div \frac{3}{10} = $ _____

8. $\frac{5}{12} \div \frac{2}{3} = $ _____

9. $\frac{14}{15} \div \frac{2}{5} = $ _____

10. $\frac{1}{3} \div \frac{3}{4} = $ _____

11. $\frac{3}{8} \div 4 = $ _____

12. $\frac{9}{10} \div \frac{3}{5} = $ _____

13. Writing to Explain Serena said that by looking for common factors and simplifying the expression, she found that $\frac{4}{10} \div \frac{5}{8} = 1\frac{9}{16}$. Do you agree with Serena? Why or why not?

$$\frac{\overset{5}{\cancel{10}}}{4} \times \frac{5}{\underset{4}{\cancel{8}}} = \frac{25}{16} = 1\frac{9}{16}$$

_____

_____

_____

14. A $\frac{5}{6}$-yard piece of fencing is made of boards that are $\frac{1}{12}$ yard wide. How many boards make up the fence?

_____

15. Nathan has $\frac{7}{8}$ lb of hummus. How many $\frac{3}{10}$-lb servings does he have?

_____

16. Algebra Which equation can you use to find the number of $\frac{1}{4}$-inch pieces that can be cut from a piece of metal $\frac{5}{8}$ of an inch long?

A $\frac{5}{8} \div \frac{1}{4} = n$

B $\frac{1}{4} \div \frac{5}{8} = n$

C $\frac{5}{8} \times \frac{1}{4} = n$

D $\frac{1}{4} \times \frac{8}{5} = n$

Estimating Quotients

Estimate each product.

1. $37\frac{1}{3} \div 5\frac{7}{8} =$ _____

2. $25\frac{1}{2} \div 6\frac{1}{4} =$ _____

3. $49\frac{4}{5} \div 6\frac{1}{2} =$ _____

4. $12\frac{3}{4} \div 5\frac{5}{9} =$ _____

5. $43\frac{2}{3} \div 5\frac{2}{5} =$ _____

6. $8\frac{1}{3} \div 2\frac{9}{10} =$ _____

7. $67\frac{1}{5} \div 7\frac{2}{7} =$ _____

8. $55\frac{5}{9} \div 7\frac{1}{6} =$ _____

9. $19\frac{6}{7} \div 4\frac{1}{8} =$ _____

10. $71\frac{4}{5} \div 7\frac{8}{9} =$ _____

11. $15\frac{7}{10} \div 3\frac{4}{9} =$ _____

12. $79\frac{4}{7} \div 8\frac{5}{8} =$ _____

13. $26\frac{1}{4} \div 2\frac{3}{8} =$ _____

14. $40\frac{8}{9} \div 7\frac{3}{5} =$ _____

15. $58\frac{1}{3} \div 19\frac{5}{6} =$ _____

16. Number Sense Tran wants to cut strips of paper that are $2\frac{1}{4}$ in. wide. His sheet of paper is $11\frac{1}{2}$ in. wide. He estimates that $11\frac{1}{2} \div 2\frac{1}{4} = 6$, so he can cut 6 strips from each sheet of paper. Is his estimate an overestimate or an underestimate? Explain.

_____

_____

17. Writing to Explain Eliza uses $2\frac{7}{8}$ feet of yarn in each gift basket she makes. Explain how to estimate how many baskets Eliza can make if she has 22 feet of yarn.

_____

_____

18. Geometry The area of this rectangle is $257\frac{1}{4}$ sq in. What is the best estimate of side length w?

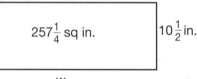

A 66,000 in.

B 50 in.

C 25 in.

D 5 in.

19. Critical Thinking What estimation method did you use to find the length of side w in Problem 18?

_____

_____

Comparing and Ordering Integers

Use <, >, or = to compare.

1. 6 ◯ −8

2. −12 ◯ −11

3. 2 ◯ |−2|

4. 12 ◯ −11

5. 11 ◯ −1

6. |−3| ◯ 4

Order from least to greatest.

7. −6, 4, 7, 0, −9 _____

8. −1, −5, 5 , 7, −8 _____

9. −7, −8, −2, 6, |−11|, −11, −9, 4, 5

_____

10. Reasoning Can any negative integer be greater than a positive integer? Explain.

_____

_____

_____

Kyle kept track of the number of points he scored each time he played a video game. Sometimes the score is less than zero.

11. Order the negative plays from least to greatest.

_____

12. Order the positive plays from greatest to least.

_____

Kyle's Scores	
Play 1:	Gained 5 points
Play 2	Lost 15 points
Play 3:	Gained 32 points
Play 4:	Gained 10 points
Play 5:	Lost 12 points
Play 6:	Lost 8 points

13. Which integer is greatest?

A 1   **B** −10   **C** 9   **D** 3

14. Writing to Explain Explain how to find the greatest integer plotted on a number line.

_____

_____

Rational Numbers on a Number Line

Write < or > in the circle.

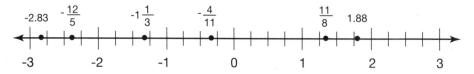

1. $-1\frac{1}{3}$ ◯ $-\frac{12}{5}$ 2. $\frac{11}{8}$ ◯ 1.88   3. $-2.8\overline{3}$ ◯ $-1\frac{1}{3}$

4. $-\frac{4}{11}$ ◯ -0.19 5. 1.6 ◯ $\frac{4}{3}$ 6. $-1/6$ ◯ -0.1

Write the numbers in order from least to greatest.

7. $0.6\overline{6}$, $-\frac{1}{3}$, $-\frac{5}{12}$ 8. $-\frac{12}{5}$, -1.35, $-1\frac{7}{9}$ 9. $\frac{3}{8}$, $\frac{2}{5}$, 0.38

_____   _____   _____

Use the table for **10** and **11**.

10. A scientist is testing lake water at different depths. Order the samples of lake water from greatest depth to least depth.

_____

Day	Feet Below the Lake Surface
Monday	$-1\frac{3}{8}$
Tuesday	-0.4
Wednesday	-1.55
Thursday	$-\frac{9}{16}$

11. **Number Sense** At what depth could the scientist take a new sample that would be shallower than the shallowest sample?

_____

12. Which rational number is least?

    A $0.6\overline{6}$

    B $-\frac{4}{5}$

    C $-\frac{6}{7}$

    D -0.6

13. **Writing to Explain** Lauren says that $-3.\overline{36}$ is greater than $-3\frac{1}{3}$. Do you agree? Explain.

_____

Name _____

Adding Integers

1. Draw a number line to find 3 + (−4).

Find each sum. Use a number line or the rules for adding integers.

2. 4 + (−12) = _____

3. −12 + (−14) = _____

4. 10 + (−1) = _____

5. −2 + (−1) = _____

6. −50 + (−1) = _____

7. 8 + (−4) = _____

8. −9 + 7 = _____

9. −3 + (−6) = _____

Algebra Use the rule to complete each table.

10. **Rule: Add -6**

Input	Output
5	
3	
−1	

11. Rule: Add 2

Input	Output
−7	
−4	
0	

12. Which is the sum of −6 + (−9) + (−9)?

A −24

B −12

C −6

D 24

13. Writing to Explain Explain how you would solve −4 + 4 + 5.

_____

_____

Subtracting Integers

For **1** through **3** use the number line below to find each difference.

1. $5 - 10$ **2.** $-4 - 4$ **3.** $6 - (-3)$

_____   _____   _____

For **4** through **9**, use a number line or the rules for adding integers to find each difference.

4. $-6 - (-1)$ **5.** $-12 - 10$ **6.** $25 - (-5)$

_____   _____   _____

7. $14 - 22$ **8.** $7 - |-6|$ **9.** $|-2| - |2|$

_____   _____   _____

For **10** through **12**, evaluate each expression for $m = -5$.

10. $52 - m$ **11.** $m - (-15)$ **12.** $18 - |-3| - m$

_____   _____   _____

13. Writing to Explain Explain when you use the word "minus" and when you use the word "negative." Give an example.

_____

_____

14. Number Sense Ben's first score on a video game was 12. His second score was -15. Which expression can he use to find how many more points he got in the first game?

   A $-12 + 15$

   B $12 - 15$

   C $12 + -15$

   D $12 - (-15)$

Multiplying Integers

1. $(-8)(-2) =$ _____

2. $7 \times (-10) =$ _____

3. $5 \times 3 =$ _____

4. $(-9)(-6) =$ _____

5. $(-6)(-3) =$ _____

6. $3 \times (-18) =$ _____

7. $-9 \times -41 =$ _____

8. $(-6)(-21) =$ _____

Number Sense Use order of operations to evaluate each expression.

9. $(-3)+ 5 + 4 - 9 \times 3 =$ _____

10. $(-6) - 4 \times 8 + 11 \times 2 =$ _____

Algebra Evaluate each expression when $r = 8$.

11. $-12r - 120 =$ _____

12. $7r + -5 =$ _____

13. $(-4r)(-30) - (-8) =$ _____

14. $(-2r)(8) + (-25) =$ _____

15. From 1950 to 1970, some glaciers thinned by an average of 1.7 ft per year. What was the change in glacier thickness during this period? _____

16. From 1995 to 2000, the glaciers thinned by 6 ft per year. What was the change in glacier thickness during this period? _____

17. Which is the product of $(-4)(-12)$?

    A -48

    B -36

    C 36

    D 48

18. Writing to Explain Explain how to evaluate $5p + (-6)$ when $p = -4$.

_____

_____

_____

_____

Name _____

Dividing Integers

Find each quotient.

1. $80 \div (-8)$ **2.** $-75 \div (-5)$ **3.** $-49 \div 7$

_____   _____   _____

4. $-45 \div (-9)$ **5.** $0 \div (-14)$ **6.** $-81 \div (-3)$

_____   _____   _____

Use order of operations to evaluate each expression for $c = -8$.

7. $-96 \div c$ **8.** $c \div 4$ **9.** $-144 \div c$

_____   _____   _____

10. $13 - (c \div 2)$ **11.** $(3c + 4) \div 5$ **12.** $c \div (-4) + 6$

_____   _____   _____

13. Reasoning Is $120 \div -6 \times -3$ positive or negative? Explain.

_____

_____

_____

14. Algebra A roller coaster dropped 224 feet in 2 seconds. What was the rate of change in height per second? Find $-224 \div 2$.

_____

15. What is the quotient of $-162 \div (-9)$?

     A -18

     B -16

     C 16

     D 18

16. Writing to Explain Jill says that the rules for multiplying and dividing integers are alike. Do you agree? Explain.

_____

_____

_____

Solving Equations with Integers

Solve and check each equation.

1. $y - (-6) = -6$

    $y = $ _____

2. $\frac{-80}{t} = 8$

    $t = $ _____

3. $-4w = -80$

    $w = $ _____

4. $u - (-96) = 2$

    $u = $ _____

5. $55 + h = -7$

    $h = $ _____

6. $n \div -9 = -9$

    $n = $ _____

7. $x + (-8) = -15$

    $x = $ _____

8. $-21c = 21$

    $c = $ _____

Reasoning Without solving, tell whether the variable is greater than, less than, or equal to -15. Tell how you decided.

9. $p + 14 = 2$

_____

_____

10. The temperature at 3:00 P.M. was $-5°F$. The temperature 1 hour later was $-8°F$. Solve the equation $-5 + d = -8$ to find the change in temperature.

                                   _____

11. A climber reached 2,500 feet up a mountain. Over the next 3 hours, she descended 600 feet down the mountain. Solve the equation $3y = -600$ to find the number of feet she descended per hour.

                                   _____

12. Which is the value of s in $s - (-87) = -120$?

    A -207 **C** 33

    B -33 **D** 207

13. **Writing to Explain** Write an equation in which the variable g stands for a negative integer. Then solve the equation for g.

_____

Name _____

Graphing Points on a Coordinate Plane

Write the ordered pair for each point.

1. F _____

2. G _____

3. H _____

4. I _____

5. J _____

6. K _____

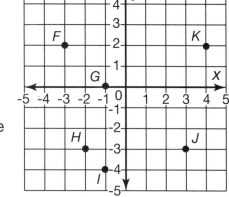

For **7** through **9**, graph the ordered pairs. Connect the points in order and describe the figure you drew.

7. (1,0), (5,0), (5, 4), (1,4)

_____

8. (0, 0), (2,−4), (−2, −4)

_____

9. (−4, −2), (−2, −2), (−2, 5), (−4, 5)

_____

10. Writing to Explain A point is located in Quadrant IV. What do you know about the signs of the coordinates for the point? Explain.

_____

_____

_____

11. Critical Thinking Draw three lines that are parallel to the x-axis. Read the ordered pairs for points on each line. What generalization can you make about the ordered pairs for lines parallel to the x-axis?

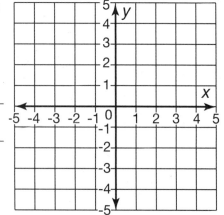

_____

_____

12. Geometry Which set of ordered pairs can be connected in order to form a right triangle?

    A (−1, 3), (−1, −1), (2, −1)

    B (−4, 0), (0, 1), (1, −2)

    C (2, 2), (2, −2), (−2, −2), (−2, 2)

    D (0, 5), (−3, 3), (3, −3)

Problem Solving: Work Backward

1. **Geometry** The volume of a rectangular prism is 208 cm^3. If the area of one end is 16 cm^2, what is the length of the prism?

_____

2. The delivery person stopped on the 14th floor to talk to a friend. Before stopping, he had just made a delivery 4 floors above. Before that he made a delivery 6 floors below. Before that he had made a delivery 9 floors above. Before that he had made a delivery 15 floors below. On what floors did he make his first delivery?

_____

3. On one day, a store sold 16 boxes of rice, restocked the shelf with 22 boxes, sold 27 boxes, restocked with 30 boxes, and sold 15 boxes. There are now 21 boxes of rice on the shelf. How many boxes were on the shelf at the start of the day?

_____

4. **Strategy Practice** Gus started with a number. He multiplied by 8, subtracted 12, divided by 4, and added 7 to get 50. Show how to work backward to find the starting number.

_____

5. At the end of the day, Brooke had $138.75 in her checking account. She had made a deposit of $115.07 and written checks totaling $176.94. How much did she have in her checking account at the beginning of the day?

   A −$76.88   **C** $200.62

   B $76.88   **D** $430.76

6. **Writing to Explain** The football team gained 7 yards, gained 4 yards, lost 5 yards, gained 21 yards, lost 2 yards, and gained 4 yards to their 43 yard line. Explain why working backward is the best strategy to use to solve this problem. Then find the yard line where the team began.

_____

_____

_____

Name _____

Basic Geometric Ideas

Use the diagram at the right. Name the following.

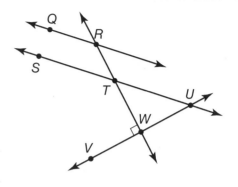

1. Two perpendicular lines _____

2. Two rays _____

3. Two parallel lines _____

4. Four line segments _____

5. Two lines that intersect _____

Draw a diagram to illustrate each situation.

6. $\overline{XY}$ with midpoint R

7. $\overline{JK}$ perpendicular to $\overline{LM}$

8. **Reasoning** How many points are shared by two
   perpendicular lines? By two parallel lines?

   _____

9. Which best describes the diagram?

   A Perpendicular lines

   B Parallel lines

   C Skew lines

   D. Intersecting lines

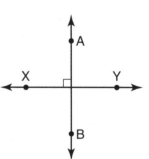

10. **Writing to Explain** In your own words, describe a plane.

_____

Name _____

Measuring and Drawing Angles

Classify each angle as acute, right, obtuse, or straight. Then measure the angle.

1.

2.

3.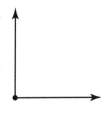

_____   _____   _____

Draw an angle for each measure.

4. 90°   **5.** 50°   **6.** 112°

Estimation Without a protractor, try to sketch an angle with the given measure. Then use a protractor to check your estimate.

7. 120°   **8.** 100°   **9.** 10°

10. Which is a measure of an acute angle?

   A 40°   **B** 90°   **C** 120°   **D** 180°

11. Writing to Explain Explain the steps you use to measure an angle using a protractor.

_____

_____

_____

Angle Pairs

For **1** through **3**, find *x*.

1.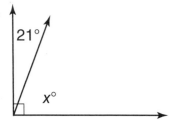

2.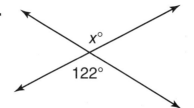

3.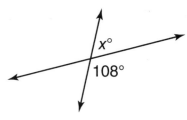

_____   _____   _____

For **4** and **5**, find the measure of an angle that is complementary to an angle with each measure.

For **6** and **7**, find the measure of an angle that is supplementary to an angle with each measure.

4. 43°   **5.** 72°   **6.** 54°   **7.** 119°

_____   _____   _____   _____

Use the diagram for **8** through **10**.

8. Name two pairs of supplementary angles.

_____

9. Name two angles adjacent to *DAE.*

_____

10. Writing to Explain How could you draw an angle complementary to ∠*DAE* without using a protractor? Tell why your method works.

_____

_____

_____

11. Critical Thinking Which statement is **NOT** true for a pair of intersecting lines?

A They form two pairs of congruent angles.

B They form four pairs of complementary angles.

C They form four pairs of supplementary angles.

D They form two pairs of vertical angles.

Triangles

Find the missing angle measure. Then classify the triangle by its angles and by its sides.

1.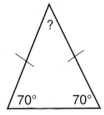
   _____

2.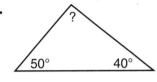
   _____

Draw the described triangle.

3. An obtuse scalene triangle

4. A triangle with a 2–inch side between two 50° angles

5. **Reasoning** Can a scalene triangle have two congruent angles? Why or why not?

_____

_____

_____

6. A right triangle has a 28° angle. What are the measures of the other angles?

   A 28° and 62°

   B 28° and 90°

   C 62° and 90°

   D 62° and 118°

7. **Writing to Explain** Are all equilateral triangles acute triangles? Explain.

_____

Quadrilaterals

Classify each polygon in as many ways as possible.

1.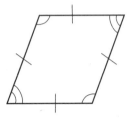

_____

_____

_____

2.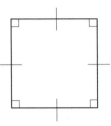

_____

_____

_____

3.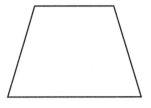

_____

_____

_____

The measures of three angles of a quadrilateral are given. Find the measure of the fourth angle and classify each quadrilateral according to its angles.

4. 125°, 55°, 125°

5. 110°, 100°, 80°

6. 90°, 70°, 150°

_____

_____

_____

_____

_____

_____

7. Draw a quadrilateral with one pair of parallel sides. One side is 1.5 in. The other side is 0.5 in. The bottom right and top right angles are 90°. The bottom left angle is 40°. Label the sides and angles.

8. A rhombus has one 65° angle and a 5 cm side. Is this enough information to find the remaining angles and side lengths? Explain.

_____

_____

9. Which pair of angles would be side-by-side in a parallelogram?

A 40°, 40°   **B** 40°, 140°   **C** 60°, 110°   **D** 65°, 105°

10. Writing to Explain What characteristics help you classify a quadrilateral as a parallelogram and not a rectangle? Explain.

_____

_____

Name _____

Circles

Identify the figure shown in bold.

1.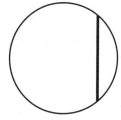

_____

2.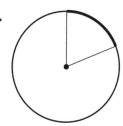

_____

3.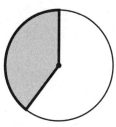

_____

4.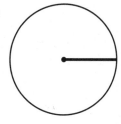

_____

5. What part of the circle is line segment *FG*?

_____

6. How many degrees are in a circle?

   A 90°

   B 120°

   C 180°

   D 360°

7. **Writing to Explain** Explain the relationship between the radius and the diameter of a circle.

_____

_____

Transformations and Congruence

1. These parallelograms are congruent.
   Find $\overline{CD}$, $\overline{GH}$, and $m\angle D$.

   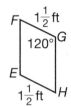 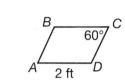

   $\overline{CD} =$ _____ $\overline{GH} =$ _____

   $m\angle D$ _____

Tell whether the figures in each pair are related by a translation, a refection, a glide reflection, or a rotation. If the relationship is a rotation, describe it.

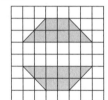   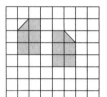   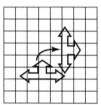

2. _____   3. _____   4. _____

5. Use the grid. Draw a semi-circle to the left of the y-axis.
   Then show the semi-circle reflected across the y-axis.

   _____

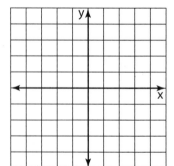

6. Cole drew two congruent polygons.
   Which is true about *all* congruent figures?

   A Corresponding angles are congruent.

   B Corresponding angles are complementary.

   C Corresponding angles are supplementary.

   D There are no corresponding angles.

7. **Writing to Explain** Draw a figure. Use different transformations of your figure to make a pattern. Show three repetitions. Then explain which transformations are used in your pattern.

   _____

Symmetry

Tell if each figure has reflection symmetry, rotational symmetry, or both. If it has reflection symmetry, how many lines of symmetry are there? If it has rotational symmetry, what is the smallest turn that will rotate the figure onto itself?

1.

2.

3.

_____   _____   _____

4. **Reasoning** Describe the symmetry of an equilateral triangle.

_____

_____

5. 808 is an example of a number with reflection symmetry.
   Write another number that has reflection symmetry.

_____

6. Which does the figure have?

   A Rotational symmetry

   B Reflection symmetry

   C Neither

   D Both

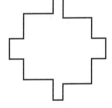

7. **Writing to Explain** Draw a figure with reflection symmetry,
   and draw the line of symmetry.

Problem Solving: Make a Table and Look for a Pattern

1. Find the next three numbers in each row. Write a formula to find any number in row B.

   _____

A	2	4	6			
B	2	8	14			

2. A company offers a 2% discount if you buy 1–5 of their products. If you buy 6–10 of their products, you earn a 3.5% discount. Buying 11–15 products will earn you a 5% discount. If the pattern continues, what discount would be offered for buying 33 products?

   _____

3. Explain the pattern. Draw the next eleven shapes.

   _____

   _____

4. In a contest, the first place team gets $\frac{1}{2}$ of the million-dollar prize. The second place team gets $\frac{1}{2}$ of the remaining money. Each team after that gets $\frac{1}{2}$ of the remaining money. How much will the sixth place team get?

   _____

5. An advertising sign lights up for 5 seconds then goes out for 2 seconds. For how many seconds will the sign be off in the first minute after the sign is turned on?

   A 46 seconds   **B** 30 seconds   **C** 16 seconds   **D** 2 seconds

6. **Writing to Explain** Explain your thinking as you find how many triangles would be in the 8th row of the pattern

   _____

   _____

   _____

Understanding Ratios

A string quartet consists of 2 violins, 1 viola, and 1 cello. Write a ratio for each comparison in three ways.

1. violins to cellos _____

2. cellos to violas _____

3. violins to all instruments _____

4. **Number Sense** How are the ratios in Exercises 1 and 2 different from the ratio in Exercise 3?

_____

_____

_____

Midland Orchards grows a large variety of apples. The orchard contains 12 rows of Granny Smith trees, 10 rows of Fuji trees, 15 rows of Gala trees, 2 rows of Golden Delicious trees, and 2 rows of Jonathan trees. Write each ratio in three ways.

5. rows of Granny Smith trees to rows of
   Golden Delicious trees _____

6. rows of Fuji trees to the total number of
   rows of trees _____

7. A grade school has 45 students who walk to school and 150 students who ride the bus. The other 50 students are driven to school. Which shows the ratio of students who walk to school to the total number of students in the school?

   A 45:50   **B** 45:195   **C** 45:150   **D** 45:245

8. **Writing to Explain** Steve said it does not matter which term is first and which term is second in a ratio, since ratios are different than fractions. Is he correct? Explain why or why not.

_____

_____

_____

Equal Ratios and Proportions

Write three ratios that are equal to the ratio given.

1. $\frac{8}{10}$ _____ **2.** $\frac{2}{3}$ _____ **3.** $\frac{3}{4}$ _____

4. 21 to 18 _____ **5.** 5 to 4 _____ **6.** 1 to 3 _____

7. 14:16 _____ **8.** 2:4 _____ **9.** 2:5 _____

Write = if the ratios form a proportion; if they do not form a proportion, write ≠.

10. 3:12 | 6:24 _____ **11.** $\frac{14}{16}$ | $\frac{7}{4}$ _____ **12.** 4 to 20 | 1 to 4 _____

Find the number that makes the ratios equivalent.

13. $\frac{8}{9}$ = _____ /36 **14.** 15:18 = 5: _____ **15.** _____ to 7 = 9 to 21

Write the ratios in simplest form.

16. $\frac{42}{28}$ _____ **17.** 21 to 36 _____ **18.** 15:45 _____

19. $\frac{35}{25}$ _____ **20.** 60 to 30 _____ **21.** 10:40 _____

22. Writing to Explain Tell why you cannot multiply or divide by zero to find equal ratios.

_____

23. Geometry Is the ratio of length to width for these two rectangles proportional? Tell how you know.

14 in. 21 in.

7 in. 15 in.

_____

24. Algebra Which value for x would make the ratios equivalent?
$\frac{3}{8} = \frac{x}{32}$

A $x = 4$

B $x = 6$

C $x = 8$

D $x = 12$

Understanding Rates and Unit Rates

Write the rate and the unit rate.

1. 42 bricks laid in 2 hours

_____

2. 15 points scored in 4 quarters

_____

3. 225 chairs in 15 rows

_____

4. 24 trees pruned in 5 days

_____

5. 480 miles in 12 hours

_____

6. $6.50 for 10 pounds

_____

7. 72 plants in 9 square feet

_____

8. 357 miles on 14 gallons

_____

9. Estimation Over 5 days, 8,208 people visited an amusement park. About how many people visited the park per day?

_____

10. Writing to Explain Explain how you could convert a rate of 18,000 miles per hour to miles per second.

_____

_____

11. Critical Thinking Matt makes 5 bookcases in 8 days. What is his unit rate?

_____

12. A space shuttle orbits Earth 1 time in 90 minutes. How many times does it orbit Earth in 6 hours?

_____

13. Which is the unit rate for 39 people in 3 vans?

   A 39 people per van

   B 13 vans per person

   C 13 people per van

   D 3 people per van

Comparing Rates

Find each unit rate and determine which rate is greater.

1. 250 mi per 10 gal or 460 mi per 20 gal

_____

2. 1,000 words in 20 min or 2,475 words in 45 min

_____

3. 6 in. of rain in 4 h or 8 in. of rain in 5 h

_____

Find each unit price and determine which is a better buy.

4. 1 lb of apples for $2.15 or 3 lb of apples for $5.76

_____

5. 8 bungee cords for $10.00 or 20 bungee cords for $22.00

_____

6. 5 oz of insect repellant for $6.95 or 14 oz of insect repellant for $19.60

_____

7. Fritz earns $75.60 for each 7-h shift that he works. Which shift pays a higher hourly wage than the wage Fritz earns?

    A $60.30 for a 6-h shift

    B $80.00 for an 8-h shift

    C $36.30 for a 3-h shift

    D $40.40 for a 4-h shift

8. Writing to Explain Shaunda said that buying 4 towels for $17 was a better buy than buying 2 towels for $9. She found her answer by doubling the terms in the ratio $\frac{9}{2}$ and comparing the first terms in the ratios. Is she correct? Use unit prices to support your answer.

_____

_____

Distance, Rate, and Time

Find the missing variable.

1. Distance = 15 mi   time = 2h   rate = _____

2. Distance = 56 km   time = 4 h   rate = _____

3. Distance = 72 yd   time = _____   rate = $\frac{12 \text{ yd}}{\text{min}}$

4. Distance = 27 cm   time = _____   rate = $\frac{3 \text{ cm}}{\text{sec}}$

5. Distance = _____   time = 2 d   rate = $\frac{5{,}000 \text{ m}}{\text{d}}$

6. Distance = _____   time = 6 wk   rate = $\frac{80 \text{ ft}}{\text{wk}}$

7. The California Speedway hosts automobile races. Which rate of speed is higher: a car completing a 500-mi race in about $3\frac{1}{3}$ h or a car completing a 300-mi race in about $2\frac{1}{2}$ h? _____

8. A train traveled 250 mi in 2 h. If it traveled at the same rate of speed, how long would it take the train to travel 600 mi? _____

9. The space shuttle travels 4,375 mi in 15 min as it orbits the earth. Estimate its average rate of speed during that time to the nearest hundred.

  A   About 400 mi per min

  B   About 300 mi per min

  C   About 60,000 mi per min

  D   About 70,000 mi per min

10. Writing to Explain Kevin drove his scooter 62 km in 2 h. Explain how to find how far he drives if he drives at the same rate for 3 h.

_____

_____

_____

Name _____

Problem Solving: Draw a Picture

Draw a picture to solve each problem.

For **1** through **3**, Pamela walks 1 mile and runs 4 miles during her daily workout.

1. What is the ratio of miles walked to miles ran during each of Pamela's workouts? _____

2. What is the ratio of miles walked to total miles in each of Pamela's workouts? _____

3. Pamela ran 20 miles last week. How many days did she workout? _____

4. There are 5 pens with blue ink, 3 pens with red ink, and 2 pens with purple ink in each package. What fraction of the pens has blue ink?

   A 5

   B $\frac{5}{5}$

   C $\frac{5}{8}$

   D $\frac{1}{2}$

5. There are 18 baseballs and basketballs in one gym storage locker. There are 3 baseballs for every 6 basketballs in the locker. How many basketballs are in the locker? _____

6. **Writing to Explain** Rasheed takes photographs with a digital camera. He estimates that for each photograph he prints, he has 5 photographs that he never prints. How many photographs has Rasheed taken if he makes 4 prints? Explain how drawing a picture can help you solve the problem. Then solve.

   _____

   _____

   _____

Name _____

Using Ratio Tables

Complete the ratio table. Add columns if needed.

1. $\dfrac{3 \text{ hops}}{5 \text{ jumps}} = \dfrac{\boxed{} \text{ hops}}{15 \text{ jumps}}$

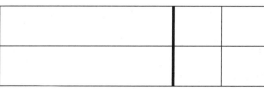

Number of hops		
Number of jumps		

_____

2. $\dfrac{\$60}{2 \text{ weeks}} = \dfrac{\$240}{\boxed{} \text{ weeks}}$

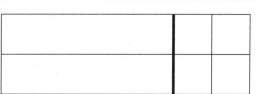

_____

3. $\dfrac{12 \text{ cans}}{7 \text{ bottles}} = \dfrac{60 \text{ cans}}{\boxed{} \text{ bottles}}$

_____

4. How many cups of loam are needed to make 66 c of potting soil?   _____

5. How many cups of humus are needed to make 11 c of potting soil?   _____

6. Sondra uses 78 c of loam to make potting soil. How many cups of humus did she use?   _____

Potting Soil for Ferns (Makes 22 c)
6 c sand
6 c loam
9 c peat moss
3 c humus
1 c dried cow manure

7. It takes Renaldo 8 h to make 7 carvings. At this rate, how many hours will it take him to make 63 carvings?

   A $7\frac{7}{8}$ h

   B 9 h

   C 56 h

   D 72 h

8. **Writing to Explain** Find three sets of values for x and y to make $\dfrac{x \text{ mi}}{y \text{ min}} = \dfrac{4 \text{ mi}}{32 \text{ min}}$ a proportion. Explain how you found the values.

   _____

   _____

Using Unit Rates

Use unit rates to solve each proportion. Estimate to check for reasonableness.

1. $\frac{a \text{ ft}}{6 \text{ h}} = \frac{20 \text{ ft}}{4 \text{ h}}$ _____

2. $\frac{36 \text{ oz}}{6 \text{ lb}} = \frac{b \text{ oz}}{4 \text{ lb}}$ _____

3. $\frac{c \text{ players}}{10 \text{ teams}} = \frac{27 \text{ players}}{3 \text{ teams}}$ _____

4. $\frac{d \text{ c}}{20 \text{ tsp}} = \frac{60 \text{ c}}{12 \text{ tsp}}$ _____

5. $\frac{e \text{ m}}{12 \text{ cm}} = \frac{63 \text{ m}}{9 \text{ cm}}$ _____

6. $\frac{16 \text{ adults}}{2 \text{ children}} = \frac{f \text{ adults}}{5 \text{ children}}$ _____

7. $\frac{\$g}{30 \text{ lawns}} = \frac{\$200}{8 \text{ lawns}}$ _____

8. $\frac{12 \text{ mL}}{6 \text{ pt}} = \frac{h \text{ mL}}{40 \text{ pt}}$ _____

9. $\frac{33 \text{ meals}}{11 \text{ days}} = \frac{k \text{ meals}}{365 \text{ days}}$ _____

10. It takes DeShawn 30 min to paint 90 feet of fence. If he paints at the same rate, how many feet of fence can he paint in 45 min? _____

11. Inez types 280 words in 7 minutes. If she types at the same rate, how many words will she type in 1 hour? _____

12. **Algebra** Explain how you can tell that $\frac{20 \text{ pens}}{2 \text{ packages}} = \frac{30 \text{ pens}}{3 \text{ packages}}$ using mental math?

_____

_____

13. Darryl was looking at the speeds of different airplanes. When he wrote a proportion to compare the speeds, he forgot to write one term. If the proportion is correct, which is the term he forgot?

$$\frac{45 \text{ mi}}{\boxed{}} = \frac{135 \text{ mi}}{12 \text{ min}}$$

A 4 mi

B 4 min

C 36 mi

D 36 min

14. **Writing to Explain** Jeanette estimates that she mails 2 letters for every 50 e-mails that she sends. She has mailed 9 letters this week. To find how many e-mails she has sent, Jeanette wrote the proportion $\frac{2 \text{ letters}}{50 \text{ e-mails}} = \frac{9 \text{ letters}}{e \text{ e-mails}}$. Tell how she can use unit rates to solve the proportion. Tell how many e-mails she received.

_____

_____

_____

_____

Ways to Solve Proportions

Use cross multiplication to solve each proportion.

1. $\frac{16 \text{ oz}}{1 \text{ lb}} = \frac{x \text{ oz}}{5 \text{ lb}}$ _____

2. $\frac{45 \text{ cm}}{15 \text{ seconds}} = \frac{60 \text{ cm}}{s \text{ seconds}}$ _____

3. $\frac{27 \text{ lessons}}{3 \text{ mo}} = \frac{n \text{ lessons}}{5 \text{ mo}}$ _____

4. $\frac{48 \text{ favors}}{12 \text{ guests}} = \frac{f \text{ favors}}{15 \text{ guests}}$ _____

5. $\frac{m \text{ min}}{3 \text{ blocks}} = \frac{32 \text{ min}}{8 \text{ blocks}}$ _____

6. $\frac{30 \text{ lb}}{5 \text{ weeks}} = \frac{54 \text{ lb}}{w \text{ weeks}}$ _____

Because each planet has a different gravitational force, the weight of objects on Earth is not the same as their weight on other planets. Use proportions to answer **7** and **8**.

7. An object that weighs 10 pounds on Earth weighs 9 pounds on Venus. How much would an object that weighs 90 pounds on Earth weigh on Venus?

_____

8. An object that weighs 234 pounds on Jupiter weighs 100 pounds on Earth. How much would an object that weighs 250 pounds on Earth weigh on Jupiter?

_____

9. **Algebra** Cecelia has read 12 books this summer and has collected 72 tokens from the library's summer reading program. Which of the following shows how to solve for the number of tokens awarded for each book?

   A $\frac{12}{72} = \frac{t}{1}$ C $\frac{12}{1} = \frac{t}{72}$

   B $\frac{12}{72} = \frac{1}{t}$ D $\frac{1}{12} = \frac{72}{t}$

10. **Writing to Explain** Explain how you would use mental math to solve this proportion. $\frac{75}{w} = \frac{1}{2}$

_____

11. **Number Sense** Are the two ratios that make up a proportion always, sometimes, or never equivalent?

_____

Problem Solving:
Writing to Explain

Explain your solution. Show your work.

1. A fundraiser is being held to raise money for a new school playground. Of every $20 raised, $16 will be spent on playground equipment. If the goal of the fundraiser is $500.00 for playground equipment, how much total money will it need to raise?

_____

_____

_____

_____

2. Stephan is planning a hiking trip at Kings Canyon National Park. He plans to hike 14 miles every 2 days. If he hikes 42 miles, how many days will he hike?

_____

_____

_____

_____

3. A rental store at the beach has 56 umbrellas and 24 surfboards. Which ratio describes the relationship of surfboards to umbrellas?

   A 56:24   **B** 7:3   **C** 3:8   **D** 3:7

4. **Writing to Explain** Kara can run 3 miles in 25.5 minutes. At this rate, how long would it take her to run 2 miles? *Diana's answer: If I subtract 1 mile from 3 miles, I get 2 miles, so if I subtract 1 minute from 25.5 minutes, I get 24.5 minutes. Kara takes 24.5 minutes to run 2 miles.* Is Diana's answer correct? Explain.

_____

_____

Similar Figures

The triangles below are similar. Use a proportion to determine the missing values.

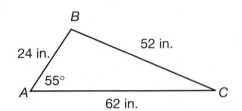
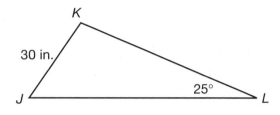

1. Find $\overline{JL}$. _____

2. Find $\overline{KL}$. _____

3. What is the measure of $\angle K$ in $\triangle JKL$ above? _____

Use the table for **4** and **5**.

	Length	Width
Rectangle *A*	14 m	12 m
Rectangle *B*	36 m	28 m
Rectangle *C*	21 m	18 m

4. Which rectangles are similar? Explain.

_____

_____

5. If a rectangle similar to Rectangle B is 12.6 m wide, how long is it?

_____

6. A scale model of a covered wagon is 3 ft long and 1 ft wide. If the actual covered wagon is 4 ft wide, what is its length?

A 7 ft   **B** 9 ft   **C** 12 ft   **D** 16 ft

7. **Writing to Explain** Draw and label a rectangle that is similar to a rectangle that is 15 cm long and 9 cm wide. Explain why the rectangles are similar.

_____

_____

Maps and Scale Drawings

Scale: 1 in. = 20 ft

0.5 in.

4.7 in.

0.5 in.

Center line

2.5 in.

2.5 in.

4.7 in.

0.5 in.

Open space

1. What is the actual length and width of a college basketball court?

_____

2. How far should open space extend from each side of the court?

_____

3. What is the actual measurement from the end of the court to the center line?

_____

4. **Reasoning** What is the scale on a map that shows two cities that are 400 mi apart as 2.5 in. apart?

_____

5. If the scale of a drawing is 1 in. = 2.5 ft, which is the actual size of an object that is 2 in. long in the drawing?

   A 1 in.   **B** 5 in.   **C** 2.5 ft   **D** 5 ft

6. **Writing to Explain** Explain how you would choose a scale to use for a map. What things would you need to consider?

_____

_____

_____

Understanding Percent

Write the percent of each figure that is shaded.

1.

_____

2.

_____

3.

_____

4.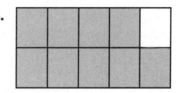

_____

5. Number Sense What percent of line segment *AB* is equal to 50% of line segment *CD*?

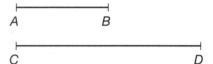

_____

6. The line segment below shows 100%. Show 25%, 50%, and 75% of the segment.

7. Which of the following figures is 60% shaded?

A   B   C   D

8. Writing to Explain You are thirsty, so a friend has offered to give you 50% of his water. What information must you have in order to find out how much water your friend will give you?

_____

_____

Name _____

Fractions, Decimals, and Percents

Describe the shaded portion of each as a fraction, decimal, and percent.

1.

2.

_____   _____

Write each in two other ways.

3. 64%   **4.** 0.09   **5.** $\frac{12}{50}$ **6.** 37%

_____   _____   _____   _____

7. $\frac{4}{250}$ **8.** 0.023

_____   _____

The table at the right shows the number of states in the United States at different times in history. There are currently 50 states in the United States. Use the information to answer the questions.

Year	States
1792	15
1817	20
1836	25
1848	30
1863	35
1889	40
1896	45
1959	50

9. In what year were there 0.5 as many states as today?

_____

10. What percent of the current number of states had joined the United States by the year 1863?

_____

11. In what year were there about $\frac{2}{3}$ as many states as in 1896? _____

12. Which of the following is equivalent to 98%?

   A 0.49   **B** $\frac{100}{98}$ **C** 0.98   **D** $\frac{49}{100}$

13. Writing to Explain Explain how you would write $\frac{5}{6}$ as a percent.

_____

Percents Greater Than 100 and Less Than 1

Write a fraction in simplest form, a decimal, and a percent to name each shaded part.

1.

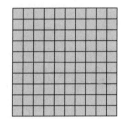

2.

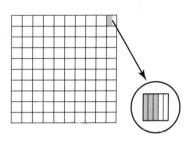

_____   _____

Write each percent as a fraction and as a decimal. Write fractions in simplest form.

3. 188% _____ ; _____   **4.** 145% _____ ; _____

5. 261% _____ ; _____   **6.** 350% _____ ; _____

7. 275% _____ ; _____   **8.** 420% _____ ; _____

9. 400% _____ ; _____   **10.** $\frac{1}{5}$% _____ ; _____

11. 0.7% _____ ; _____   **12.** $\frac{1}{3}$% _____ ; _____

13. The land area of Yosemite National Park is 3079 km^2. This is about 189% of the land area of Sequoia National Park. Write 189% as a fraction in simplest form and as a decimal.

A $\frac{100}{189}$, 0.53 (rounded)   **C** $\frac{189}{100}$, 18.9

B $\frac{189}{100}$, 1.89   **D** $\frac{3079}{189}$, 16.29

14. Writing to Explain Nathan wanted to save $400 for a new bicycle. He save 110% of his goal amount. Write 110% as a fraction in simplest form and as a decimal. Has he saved enough money to buy the bicycle? Explain how you know.

_____

_____

_____

_____

Estimating Percent

Estimate.

1. 35% of 102 _____

2. 42% of 307 _____

3. 79% of 13 _____

4. 84% of 897 _____

5. 13% of 97 _____

6. 28% of 95 _____

7. 61% of 211 _____

8. 19% of 489 _____

9. 48% of 641 _____

10. 21% of 411 _____

11. 77% of 164 _____

12. 51% of 894 _____

13. 39% of 306 _____

14. 62% of 522 _____

15. 48% of 341 _____

16. **Number Sense** Which would you need to estimate to find an answer, 45% of 200 or 46% of 97?

_____

17. The school store sold 48 items on Monday. Of those items, 60% were pens. About how many pens were sold on Monday?

_____

18. The school cafeteria workers cooked 52 lb of pasta on Thursday. Of that, 90% was sold on Thursday, and 10% was stored in the refrigerator. About how much pasta was stored in the refrigerator?

_____

19. On a rainy day, 76% of the students in the school brought umbrellas. There are 600 students in the school. About how many students brought umbrellas?

_____

20. Which of the following is the best estimate for 68% of 251?

    A 150

    B 175

    C 204

    D 210

21. **Writing to Explain** Explain how you would estimate 79% of 389.

_____

_____

_____

_____

_____

Name _____

Finding the Percent of a Number

Find the percent of each number.

1. 42% of 800 _____   **2.** 5.6% of 425 _____   **3.** 85% of 15 _____

4. $33\frac{1}{3}$% of 678 _____   **5.** 12% of 65 _____   **6.** 58% of 324 _____

7. 98% of 422 _____   **8.** 32% of 813.5 _____   **9.** 78% of 219 _____

10. 13% of 104 _____   **11.** 24% of 529 _____   **12.** 4.5% of 82 _____

13. 64% of 912 _____   **14.** 128% of 256 _____   **15.** 63% of 1,368 _____

16. About 42% of the flag of the United States is red.
On a flag that is 9 feet tall and 15 feet wide, how
many square feet are red?   _____

17. **Estimation** Estimate 68% of 32, then find the   _____
actual answer. Which is greater?

_____

For **18** and **19**, round your answer to the nearest whole number.

18. An adult has 206 bones. Of those, approximately 2.9% are found
in the inner ear. About how many bones in the human body are
found in the inner ear?

_____

19. Approximately 12.6% of the bones are vertebrae in the human
back. About how many bones in the human body are vertebrae?

_____

20. 45 is 12% of which number?

  A 540   **B** 450   **C** 375   **D** 5.4

21. **Writing to Explain** Without calculating, tell which is greater, 52%
of 3,400 or 98% of 1,500. Explain.

_____

_____

Name _____

Tips, Taxes, Discount, and Simple Interest

Find the sale price or total cost.

1. Regular Price: $125
Discount: 15%
Sale Price: _____

2. Subtotal: $135
Sales Tax: 8%
Total Cost: _____

3. Subtotal: $62.50
Tip: 20%
Total Cost: _____

4. Regular Price: $98
Discount: 12%
Sale Price: _____

5. Subtotal: $75.25
Sales Tax: 7.5%
Total Cost: _____

6. Subtotal: $48.79
Tip: 15%
Total Cost: _____

7. Sam bought a video game system for $250 on the store credit plan. The credit plan charges 8.5% interest per year. How much money will Sam need to pay for the system if he pays it off in one year?

_____

8. Algebra Tara's bank account earned $11.25 in interest on a deposit she made one year ago. Her account pays a simple interest rate of 4.5%. How much money did Tara deposit in her account?

_____

9. Janine bought a portable CD player for $75. If the sales tax is 5%, what is the total cost of the CD player?

A $70.00

B $71.25

C $78.75

D $80.00

10. Writing to Explain Thom wants to buy a $65 radio. He has a coupon for 25% off. If Thom has $50 and the sales tax is 6%, does he have enough to buy the radio? Explain.

_____

_____

_____

Problem Solving: Reasonableness

Look back and check. Tell if the answer given is reasonable.
Explain why or why not.

1. A shipment of 200 games is 20% video games, 50% board games,
   and 30% puzzles. How many board games are chess if 25% of the
   board games are chess?
   Answer: The number of chess games is 50.

   _____

   _____

2. A DVD player costs $199. How much will it cost if it is 15% off?
   Answer: The cost of the DVD player will be $169.15.

   _____

   _____

3. **Write a Problem** An ad in the newspaper is offering 25% off
   ski lift tickets at Big Bear. The original tickets cost $60. Write a
   problem using the information from the ad. Then give an answer
   for someone to look back and check for reasonableness.

   _____

   _____

4. Students at Warm Springs Middle School are going on a field trip
   to Orange County. If 60% of the 120 students signed up for the
   field trip are girls, and 25% of the girls are in sixth grade, how
   many sixth grade girls are going on the field trip?

   A 18   **B** 25   **C** 43   **D** 102

5. **Writing to Explain** Bailey paid $42 for a backpack that was 40%
   off the original price. Is $56 a reasonable price for the original cost
   of the backpack? Explain.

   _____

   _____

Equations with More Than One Operation

1. $12a + 24 = 48$ _____

2. $4z - 8 = 32$ _____

3. $\frac{x}{5} - 10 = 2$ _____

4. $\frac{p}{3} + 6 = 42$ _____

5. $5b + 15 = 30$ _____

6. $7n + 14 = 21$ _____

7. $\frac{c}{4} + 3 = 5$ _____

8. $\frac{q}{2} - 4 = 18$ _____

9. $17 + 3y = 38$ _____

10. $\frac{m}{4} - 17 = 4$ _____

11. $\frac{c}{12} + 12 = 21$ _____

12. $8z - 13 = 7$ _____

For **13** and **14**, write and solve an equation.

13. Yoshi's age is twice Bart's age plus 3. Yoshi is 13 years old. How old is Bart?

_____

14. Caleb and Winona both travel by car to their friend's home. The distance Winona traveled was 124 miles less than twice the distance Caleb traveled. If Winona traveled 628 miles, how far did Caleb travel?

_____

15. Critical Thinking Explain the mistake in this solution and find the correct solution.

$$6x + 15 = 69$$
$$6x = 84$$
$$x = 14$$

_____

_____

16. Number Sense Which is the value of n when $4n + 16 = 64$?

A $n = 4$ **B** $n = 8$ **C** $n = 12$ **D** $n = 16$

17. Writing to Explain Explain how to solve the equation $6x - 3 = 39$.

_____

_____

Patterns and Equations

Write a rule and an equation to fit the pattern in each table in **1** through **6**.

1.

x	−2	−1	0	1	2
y	3	4	5	6	7

_____

_____

2.

x	−6	−3	12	21	36
y	−2	−1	4	7	12

_____

_____

3.

x	4	7	11	14	17
y	−4	−1	3	6	9

_____

_____

4.

x	−2	−1	0	1	2
y	−8	−4	0	4	8

_____

_____

5.

x	3	9	13	22	27
y	10	16	20	29	34

_____

_____

6.

x	−2	−1	2	3	4
y	6	3	−6	−9	−12

_____

_____

7. The Gadget Factory sells winkydiddles in different quantities, as shown by the table. How much would ten winkydiddles cost?

Number of Winkydiddles	7	12	26	31
Cost	$24.50	$42.00	$91.00	$108.50

_____

8. Which equation best describes the pattern in the table?

x	4	9	12	16	19
y	2	4.5	6	8	9.5

A $y = (-1)x$ **B** $y = x - 1$ **C** $y = \frac{x}{2}$ **D** $y = x + 1$

9. Writing to Explain All the values of x in a table are greater than the corresponding values of y. If x is a positive integer, what operation(s) and circumstance(s) could explain this pattern?

_____

_____

Name _____

More Patterns and Equations

In **1** through **4,** use the equation given to complete each table.

1. $y = 2x + 4$

x	0	1	2	3
y				

2. $y = 4x - 3$

x	−2	0	2	4
y				

3. $y = 100 - 4x$

x	2	4	6	8
y				

4. $y = \frac{1}{3}x + 1$

x	−3	0	3	6
y				

5. Writing to Explain Complete the table and write an equation for the pattern. Tell how you do it.

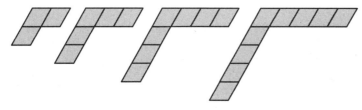

Pattern Number, p	1	2	3	4
Number of Blocks, b	3			

_____

_____

6. Algebra How many blocks are needed to make the 10th figure in the pattern above?

A 11 **B** 20 **C** 21 **D** 22

7. Reasoning Justin used 35 blocks to make a figure for the pattern above. What was the pattern number for the figure? _____

8. Write a Problem Write a problem that can be represented by this equation and table.

$y = 20x + 5$

x	1	2	3	4
y	25	45	65	85

_____

Graphing Equations

For **1** and **2**, make a T-table. Then graph each equation.

1. $y = x - 3$

2. $y = -2x$

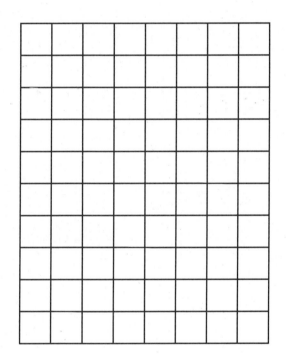 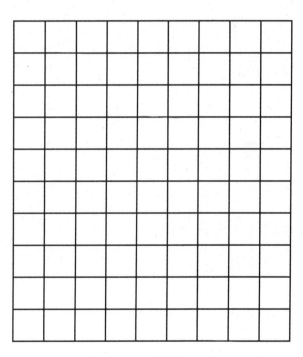

3. Reasoning Is the point (5, 6) on the graph for the
equation $y = -2x + 5$? _____

4. Which point is on the graph for the equation $y = -14 + x$?

   A (1, 5)

   B (2, 12)

   C (−2, −16)

   D (−7, 21)

5. Writing to Explain Explain how making a T-table helps you graph an equation.

_____

_____

Graphing Equations with More Than One Operation

For **1** and **2**, make a T-table and graph each equation.

1. $y = 3x - 5$

x	y

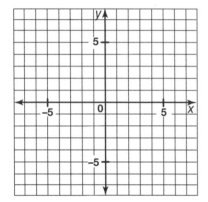

2. $y = 2x + 2$

x	y

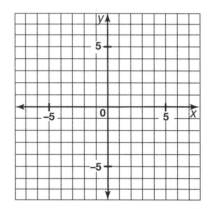

3. Which equation is shown by the graph?

A $y = 2x - 1$

B $y = x - 1$

C $y = 2x + 1$

D $y = x + 1$

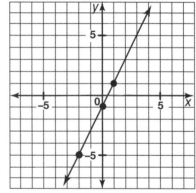

4. Writing to Explain Carrie says that one solution to $y = 3x - 5$ is (4, 7). Describe two ways to check if her statement is true. Use at least one way to check her answer.

_____

_____

Name _____

Functions

Tell whether each relation shown in the table is a function.

1.

x	y
0	−1
1	1
0	2
2	3

_____

2.

x	y
3	−2
5	0
7	2
12	7

_____

3.

x	y
0	8
5	13
10	18
15	23

_____

4. Draw a graph for the table. Do the ordered pairs represent a function? Explain.

x	y
1	−1
2	0
3	1
4	2

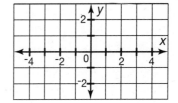

_____

_____

_____

5. Which relation shown in the table is **NOT** a function?

A

x	−2	0	2	4
y	2	4	6	8

C

x	12	9	6	3
y	3	0	−3	−6

B

x	5	10	15	20
y	11	21	31	41

D

x	3	3	4	5
y	−1	1	−1	1

6. **Writing to Explain** Gabriel says that the equation $y = 3x$ represents a function. Explain why Gabriel is correct.

_____

_____

_____

_____

_____

Problem Solving: Act It Out and Use Reasoning

1. A ranch owner has 18 bales of hay to distribute in 3 cow pastures and 3 horse pastures. He wants each cow pasture to have the same number of bales of hay and each horse pasture to have the same number of bales of hay. He wants at least 1 bale of hay in each pasture. How many different ways can hay be distributed among the pastures? Make a table to show your reasoning.

_____

2. A nursery has 10 tree seedlings to give out at 2 workshops. It wants to give out a minimum of 2 seedlings at each workshop. How many different ways can the nursery give out seedlings? Show your answer as ordered pairs.

_____

_____

3. Graph the solution to the tree seedling problem above.

4. A reading club at a bookstore gives a certificate for one free book after the reader earns 150 points. Each book a person reads is worth 3 points. Sonja has 96 points. What is the least number of books she needs to read to get the certificate?

   A 18

   B 23

   C 23

   D 54

5. **Writing to Explain** Explain how you know you found all of the possible ways to distribute the bales of hay in Problem 1.

   _____

   _____

   _____

Converting Customary Measures

Complete.

1. 3.5 ft = _____ in.   2. 17 yd = _____ ft

3. 1.5 gal = _____ c   4. 4 mi = _____ ft

5. 160 fl oz = _____ qt   6. 72 in. = _____ ft

7. 3 mi = _____ yd   8. 12 pt = _____ qt

9. 180 ft = _____ yd   10. 2 gal = _____ fl oz

11. How many tons are in 35,000 lb? _____

12. **Number Sense** Brian pole vaulted over a bar that was 189 in. high. How many more inches would he need to vault to go over a bar that was 16 ft high?

_____

A paving company was hired to make a 4 mile section of the highway. They need 700 tons of concrete to complete the job.

13. How many yards of highway do they need to repave?

_____

14. How many pounds of concrete will they need to repave the highway?

_____

15. Gary's cat weighs 11 lb. How many ounces is that?

   A 132   **B** 144   **C** 164   **D** 176

16. **Writing to Explain** The average car manufactured in the United States in 2001 could drive 24.5 mi on 1 gal of gas. Explain how to find the number of yards the car can travel on 1 gal of gas.

_____

_____

_____

Converting Metric Measures

Name the most appropriate metric unit for each measurement.

1. mass of a paperclip

_____

2. capacity of a water cooler

_____

3. width of a sheet of paper

_____

Complete.

4. 2.7 m = _____ cm

5. 1.6 kg = _____ g

6. 9 L = _____ mL

7. 14 m = _____ mm

8. 1.6 cm = _____ mm

9. 5,400 g = _____ kg

10. 1,840 mL = _____ L

11. 32 km = _____ m

12. Number Sense The chemist needs 2,220 mL of potassium chloride to complete an experiment. He has 2 L. Does he have enough to complete the experiment? Explain.

_____

13. A computer floppy disk has a mass of 20 g. How many would you need to have a total mass of 1 kg?

_____

14. A battery is 5 cm long. How many batteries would you need to line up to get 3 m?

_____

15. Which would you do to convert 25 cm to millimeters?

A Divide by 10

C Multiply by 10

B Divide by 100

D Multiply by 100

16. Writing to Explain A banana has a mass of 122 g. Explain how to find the mass of the banana in milligrams.

_____

_____

_____

Units of Measure and Precision

Measure each line to the nearest $\frac{1}{8}$ inch and to the nearest centimeter.

1. _____

_____

2. _____

_____

3. _____

_____

4. _____

_____

Measure each line segment to the nearest $\frac{1}{16}$ inch and to the nearest millimeter.

5. _____

_____

6. _____

_____

7. _____

_____

8. _____

_____

9. The mast of a sailboat was measured at 14.5 feet, 14.48 feet, and 14 feet $5\frac{3}{16}$ inches. Which is the most precise measurement? Why?

_____

10. A Maui's Dolphin is measured at 9.4 meters. Name three units of measure that would be more precise than the unit used to measure the dolphin.

_____

11. The doctor prescribed some powdered medicine in 3-centigram doses. The pharmacist prepared the medicine by measuring each dose in milligrams. Which measure is most precise? Why?

_____

12. You can buy soup measured in cups, fluid ounces, pints, or quarts. Which measure would give you the most precise measurement?

A cups   **B** pints   **C** ounces   **D** quarts

13. **Writing to Explain** Which would be a more precise unit of measure: 1 cm or 1 mm? Explain your reasoning.

_____

_____

Relating Customary and Metric Measures

Complete. Round to the nearest tenth.

1. 100 cm ≈ _____ in.

2. 16.5 gal ≈ _____ L

3. 24.8 kg ≈ _____ lb

4. 375 yd ≈ _____ m

5. 11.5 ft ≈ _____ cm

6. 24 oz ≈ _____ g

7. Estimation Use 1 t ≈ 1.1 T to estimate the number of tons in 10 t. _____

8. Reasoning If a recipe calls for 4 c of milk, and you have 1 L of milk, would it be enough? _____

Convert each. Round to the nearest tenth.

9. The number of feet in the 200 m race _____

10. The number of miles in the 5,000 m race _____

11. The number of miles in the 20 km race _____

12. The phrase *800 lb gorilla* means you are facing a tough task. How might you change this phrase to express it in metric terms?

_____

_____

13. Sarah has 2L of milk. How many quarts of milk is this?

A 2.1   **B** 2.11   **C** 2.12   **D** 21.12

14. Writing to Explain Billy wants to ride the roller coaster. A sign says he must be 138 cm tall. Explain how Billy can convert the measurement to feet and inches.

_____

_____

_____

Time

Find each elapsed time.

1. Start: 1:26 A.M.
   End: 4:31 A.M.

   _____

2. Start: 2:08 P.M.
   End: 11:43 P.M.

   _____

3. Start: 5:16 A.M.
   End: 8:00 A.M.

   _____

4. Start: 9:38 P.M.
   End: 1:16 A.M.

   _____

5. Start: 12:04 A.M.
   End: 1:37 P.M.

   _____

6. Start: 5:27 P.M.
   End: 12:00 P.M.

   _____

Find the start time or the end time using the given elapsed time.

7. Start: 4:58 P.M.
   Elapsed: 2 h 37 min

   _____

8. End: 6:31 A.M.
   Elapsed: 3 h 40 min

   _____

9. Start: 8:22 A.M.
   Elapsed: 6 h 5 min

   _____

10. End: 9:00 P.M.
   Elapsed: 5 h 19 min

   _____

11. Start: 11:42 A.M.
   Elapsed: 4 h 45 min

   _____

12. End: 12:22 A.M.
   Elapsed: 7 h 51 min

   _____

13. In 1990, Gary Stewart of California set a world record by
making 177,737 consecutive jumps on a pogo stick in 20 hours
20 minutes. If he began at 10:30 A.M. on Tuesday, at what time did
he stop?

_____

14. The play began at 7:30 P.M., and included two 20-minute
intermissions. If the play lasts 2 hours 35 minutes, at what
time did the play end?

   A 9:45 P.M.   **B** 9:55 P.M.   **C** 10:25 P.M.   **D** 10:45 P.M.

15. **Writing to Explain** Sara leaves home for work at 6:55 A.M. She gets home after work
at 5:10 P.M. Explain what must be considered in finding how long she spends away
from home. Then solve the problem.

_____

_____

_____

Problem Solving:
Use Reasoning

Robert made a number line game with three sizes of jumps: small, medium, and large.

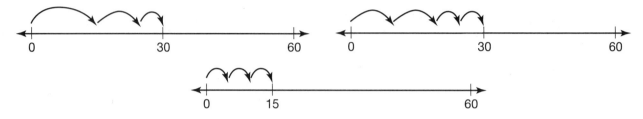

1. How many units are in each size of jump?

   _____

   _____

2. Kurt landed on 20 and wants to get to 60 in the fewest jumps possible without going past 60. Which combination of jumps should he take?

   A   8 small jumps

   B   3 medium jumps and 2 small jumps

   C   2 large jumps and 1 medium jump

   D   1 large jump, 2 medium jumps, and 1 small jump

3. Monique landed on 35. What are two ways she can get to 60 in exactly three jumps.

   _____

4. How can you get from 0 to 60 in exactly seven jumps if you use at least one jump of each size?

   _____

5. **Writing to Explain** Harvey has a 3-qt container and a 5-qt container. How can he measure exactly 4 qt of water?

   _____

   _____

   _____

   _____

Name _____

Perimeter

Find the perimeter of each figure.

1. rectangle

length 6 in., width 14 in.

_____

2. regular pentagon

sides 3.3 cm long

_____

3. regular octagon

sides $8\frac{3}{4}$in. long

_____

Estimate the perimeter of each figure. Then find the perimeter.

4.
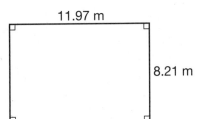
11.97 m

8.21 m

_____

5.
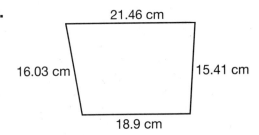
21.46 cm

16.03 cm

15.41 cm

18.9 cm

_____

Find the length of each unknown side. Then find the perimeter.

6.
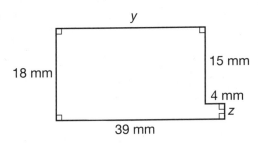
y

18 mm

15 mm

4 mm

z

39 mm

_____

_____

7.
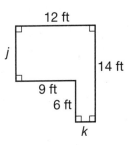
12 ft

j

14 ft

9 ft

6 ft

k

_____

_____

8. One side of a regular hexagon is 18 cm. Which is the perimeter?

A 108 cm

B 96 cm

C 72 cm

D 36 cm

9. Writing to Explain A square and a rectangle each have
a perimeter of 100 ft. Explain how this is possible.

_____

_____

Area of Rectangles and Irregular Figures

Find the area of each figure.

1.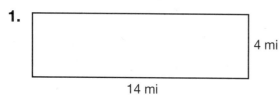

4 mi

14 mi

2.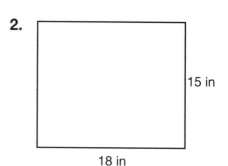

15 in

18 in

3.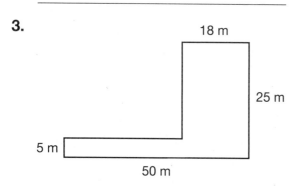

18 m

25 m

5 m

50 m

4.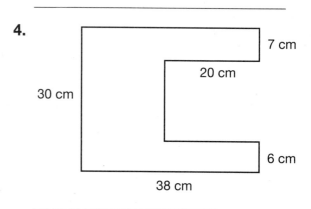

7 cm

20 cm

30 cm

6 cm

38 cm

For **5** and **6**, draw and label the figures described using graph paper. Then calculate the area of each figure.

5. A rectangle that is 13 units by 9 units

_____

6. Carlos is laminating a kitchen counter that has dimensions of 12 feet by 3 feet. The counter has a hole with dimensions of 3 feet by 2 feet cut in it for a sink. What is the area of the kitchen counter that Carlos will laminate?

_____

7. What is the area of a square that is 30 centimeters on one side?

A 60 cm^2 **B** 120 cm^2 **C** 300 cm^2 **D** 900 cm^2

8. Writing to Explain If you know the perimeter of a rectangle but not its length or width, can you calculate its area? Explain.

_____

_____

Area of Parallelograms and Triangles

Find the area of each parallelogram or triangle.

1.

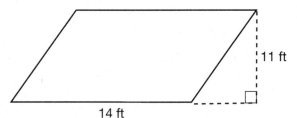

11 ft

14 ft

2.

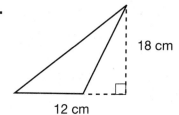

18 cm

12 cm

_____   _____

3. Triangle
$b = 30$ m
$h = 15$ m

4. Parallelogram
$b = 18$ in.
$h = 2$ ft

5. Triangle
$b = 20$ ft
$h = 3$ yd

_____   _____   _____

6. Writing to Explain The area of a triangle is 42 square inches. The triangle's base is 6 inches. Find the height of the triangle. Explain how you do it.

_____

_____

7. Number Sense A parallelogram has a base of 4 m and a height of 3 m. Find the area of the parallelogram in square centimeters.

_____

8. Estimation Which is the best estimate of the area of a triangle that has a base of 23.62 cm and a height of 8.33 cm?

A 200 cm^2 **B** 160 cm^2 **C** 100 cm^2 **D** 50 cm^2

9. Reasoning The area of a figure is 36 cm^2. Give 4 possible shapes of the figure. Where possible give 3 possible sets of dimensions for each possible shape.

_____

_____

_____

_____

Name _____

Circumference

Find each circumference. Use 3.14 or $\frac{22}{7}$ for π.

1.

29 ft

_____

2.

12 cm

_____

3.

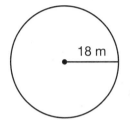

18 m

_____

4.

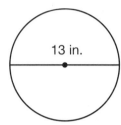

13 in.

_____

Find the missing measurement for each circle. Round to the nearest hundredth.

5. $C = 60.288$ cm, $d =$ _____   **6.** $C = 11.304$ m, $r =$ _____

7. Estimation CD's have a diameter of about 5 in. Estimate the circumference of a CD.

_____

8. Angela baked an apple pie that had a radius of 6 in. She wants to cut the pie into eight equal slices. How wide will each piece of pie be at the outer edge?

A 5.2 in.   **B** 4.7 in.   **C** 4.4 in.   **D** 4.2 in.

9. Writing to Explain Based on the diagram, is it correct to say that the smaller circle has one half the circumference of the larger. Why?

_____

_____

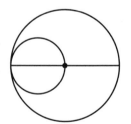

_____

Area of a Circle

Find the area of each circle to the nearest whole number.
Use 3.14 or $\frac{22}{7}$ for π.

1.
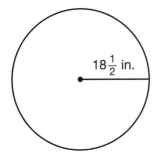

$18\frac{1}{2}$ in.

_____

2.
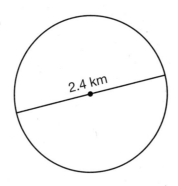

2.4 km

_____

3.
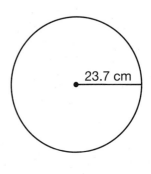

23.7 cm

_____

4. $d = 14$ in.

_____

5. $r = 11.25$ cm

_____

6. $d = 2$ mi

_____

Brian's dad wants to put a circular pool in their backyard. He can choose between pools with diameters of 15 ft, 17 ft, or 22 ft. Round to the nearest square foot.

7. How many more square feet would the 17 ft pool use than the 15 ft pool?

_____

8. How many more square feet would the 22 ft pool use than the 17 ft pool?

_____

9. On a water ride at the amusement park, a rotating valve sprays water for 15 ft in all directions. What is the area of the circular wet patch it creates?

A 30 ft^2

B 31.4 ft^2

C 94.2 ft^2

D 706.5 ft^2

10. Writing to Explain Explain how to find the radius of a circle with an area of 50.24 mi.

_____

_____

_____

Problem Solving: Use Objects

Fit two pentominoes together to create each shape. Draw the pentominoes used in each figure.

1.

2.

3. What is the area in square units of each figure you made in Problems 1 and 2?

_____

4. Tessa used pentominoes to make this rectangle. The I pentomino is shown. What is the area of the rectangle in square units?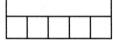

    A 5 square units   **C** 20 square units

    B 6 square units   **D** 25 square units

5. Use nine pentominoes to make a figure that is three times the size of the pentomino below. Two pentominoes have been placed to get you started. Write the perimeter and the area of both figures.

X

$A =$ _____ $P =$ _____ $A =$ _____ $P =$ _____

6. **Writing to Explain** Circle the pentominoes. Explain why any figures are not pentominoes.

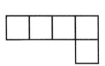   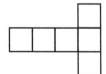

_____

_____

_____

_____

Solid Figures

Classify the polyhedron. Name all vertices, edges, faces, and bases.

1. 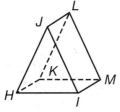 _____

_____

_____

_____

_____

Classify each figure.

2.

3.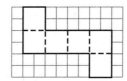

4.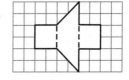

_____ _____ _____

5. Which solid figure looks like a round cake? _____

6. Number Sense How many faces make up six number cubes? _____

7. Reasoning A factory buys the boxes it needs in the form of flat nets. What advantages might the factory have in doing this?

_____

_____

8. What is the name of the polyhedron shown below?

   A Rectangular prism

   B Hexagonal prism

   C Pentagonal prism

   D Octagonal prism

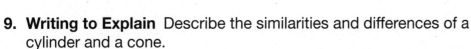

9. Writing to Explain Describe the similarities and differences of a cylinder and a cone.

_____

_____

Name _____

Surface Area

Find the surface area of each figure.

1.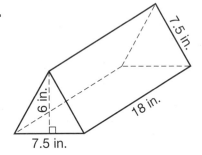

7.5 in.

7.5 in.

6 in.

18 in.

_____

2.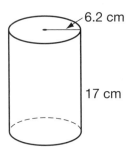

6.2 cm

17 cm

_____

3.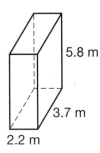

5.8 m

3.7 m

2.2 m

_____

Find the surface area of each rectangular prism.

4. l = 6.9 mm, w = 8.2 mm, h = 14 mm   _____

5. l = 3.4 cm, w = 12.7 cm, h = 16.5 cm   _____

6. l = 5.7 yd, w = 9 yd, h = 12.9 yd   _____

7. Reasoning Margaret wants to cover a footrest in the shape of a
rectangular prism with cotton fabric. The footrest is 18 in. × 12 in. ×
10 in. She has 1 yd^2 of fabric. Can she completely cover the footrest?

_____

_____

_____

8. Which is the surface area of a rectangular prism with a length of
2.3 in., a width of 1.1 in., and a height of 3 in.?

A 26.48 in^2 **B** 25.46 in^2 **C** 24.58 in^2 **D** 21.5 in^2

9. Writing to Explain A square pyramid has 2 m sides on the base.
Each face is a triangle with a base of 2 m and a height of 1.5 m.
Explain how to find the surface area.

_____

_____

_____

120

Name _____

Volume of Rectangular Prisms

Find the volume of each rectangular prism.

1. 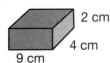 2 cm 4 cm 9 cm

2. 5 in. 6 in. 3 in.

3. 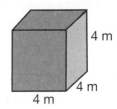 4 m 4 m 4 m

_____   _____   _____

Find the missing value for each rectangular prism.

4. Volume = 6 cu in.
Length = 3 in.
Width = 2 in.
Height = _____

5. Volume = 96 cu yd
Length = _____
Width = 6 yd
Height = 8 yd

6. Volume = 125 cu ft
Length = 5 ft
Width = _____
Height = 5 ft

7. Number Sense Suppose a box has a volume of 1 cu yd.
What is its volume in cubic feet? _____

8. A rectangular prism has a base of 12 cm^2, a length of 3 cm, a width
of 4 cm, and a height of 10 cm. Which is the volume of the prism?

A 36 cm^3

B 48 cm^3

C 120 cm^3

D 1,440 cm^3

9. Writing to Explain Find and compare the volumes of the two
rectangular prisms below. How does doubling the measure of each
dimension in a rectangular prism change the volume of the prism?

	Length	Width	Height	Volume
Rectangular Prism 1	5 ft	2 ft	10 ft	
Rectangular Prism 2	10 ft	4 ft	20 ft	

_____

_____

Volume of Triangular Prisms and Cylinders

Find the volume of each solid. Round answers to the nearest tenth.

1.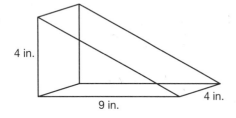

4 in.

9 in.

4 in.

_____

2.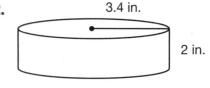

3.4 in.

2 in.

_____

3.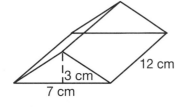

12 cm

3 cm

7 cm

_____

4.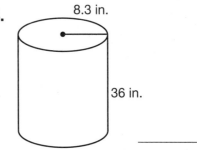

8.3 in.

36 in.

_____

5. Number Sense Compare the volume of a rectangular prism that has a square base 5 in. on a side and a height of 8 in. with the volume of a cylinder that has a base with a diameter of 5 in. and a height of 8 in.

_____

_____

6. A specialty cooking oil is packaged in a bottle that is a triangular prism. The base of the bottle is 2.2 in. wide and 2.4 in. high; the bottle is 6 in. tall. The glass is 0.2 in. thick. What is the interior volume of the bottle?

_____

7. Writing to Explain Is it correct to write the volume of a 6-cm-tall cylinder with a radius of 4 cm as "$V = 150.72$ cm^3"? Explain.

_____

_____

_____

Problem Solving:
Use Objects and Reasoning

Find the volume and surface area of each figure of centimeter cubes.

1.

_____

2.

_____

3.

_____

4.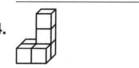

_____

5.

_____

6.

_____

7. Make a figure of cubes that has a
volume of 6 cm^3 and a surface area
of 22 cm^2. Draw your figure.

8. **Critical Thinking** Without building a model, tell whether a long row of 8 cubes or
a cube made from 8 cubes would have a greater surface area. Explain.

_____

_____

9. Make a figure that has the same
volume as the diagram, but a greater
surface area. Draw your figure.

10. **Writing to Explain** Find the volume and surface area of these figures. Then describe
the pattern(s) you see. Can you determine the volume of the next element
in the pattern? The surface area? Explain.

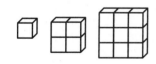

_____

_____

Name _____

Reading and Making Graphs

Use the double-bar graph for **1** through **3**.

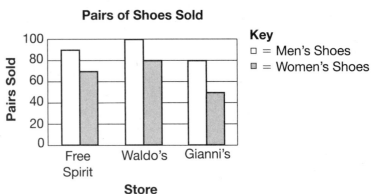

Pairs of Shoes Sold

Key
□ = Men's Shoes
■ = Women's Shoes

1. Which shoe store sold the greatest number of men's shoes?

   _____

2. **Number Sense** How many more pairs of men's shoes did Free Spirit sell than Gianni's?

   _____

3. Use the data in the table to complete the double-line graph below.

	Jan	Feb	Mar	Apr	May	Jun	Jul	Aug	Sep	Oct	Nov	Dec
Stock A	$17	$10	$10	$16	$17	$14	$12	$8	$6	$7	$11	$11
Stock B	$33	$27	$26	$28	$31	$29	$28	$20	$12	$13	$13	$14

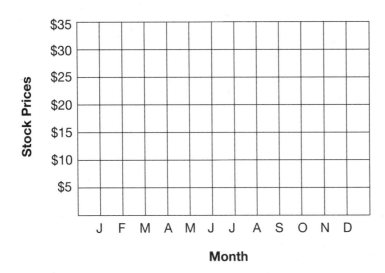

Key
■ = Stock A
● = Stock B

Month

4. Between which two months did the price of Stock A change the least?

   A February and March   **C** June and July

   B August and September   **D** September and October

5. **Writing to Explain** Explain how the trends are similar for the stocks.

   _____

   _____

124

Circle Graphs

The circle graph shows the amount the Johnson family
will spend on different categories this year. The total
amount of their budget is $10,000.

Expenses

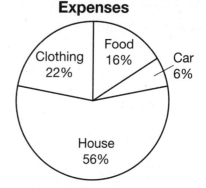

1. In which category will the Johnson family spend
   the most?

   _____

2. How much will be spent on clothing?

   _____

3. How much will be spent on food?   _____

4. **Estimation** Estimate the amount of money that
   will be spent on the house.   _____

5. Make a circle graph of the data given in the table.

Books Sold

Mystery	2,035
Western	407
Science Fiction	2,442
Adventure	3,256
TOTAL	8,140

6. Jane spent 62% of her school budget on books. In degrees,
   what measurement would that section be on a circle graph?

   A 62°   **B** 162°   **C** 177°   **D** 223°

7. Jane has a budget of $290. Explain how you would find the
   amount Jane spent on books.

   _____

   _____

Comparing Graphs

A survey asked 500 people which type of nut they preferred. The results are shown in the bar graph and circle graph. Use the graphs for **1** and **2**.

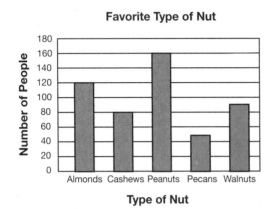

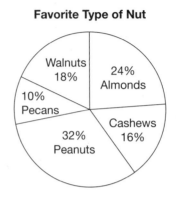

1. **Reasoning** A store manager uses the graphs to buy fresh nuts for the store. Which graph would be most helpful in deciding how many pounds of each type of nut to buy? Explain.

   _____

   _____

2. **Number Sense** Which three types of nuts combine to make about $\frac{3}{4}$ of the favorite types of nuts? Explain.

   _____

   _____

Use the graph for **3** and **4**.

3. **Writing to Explain** Explain why this claim is misleading: "Attendance at tennis games in 2008 is 50% less than in 2005."

   _____

   _____

   _____

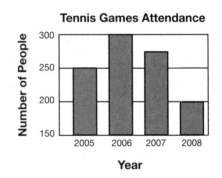

4. If the claim were true, what would have been the attendance in 2008?

   A 50   **C** 125

   B 100   **D** 150

Problem Solving: Make a Graph

1. What kind of graph would you make to show the amount in your savings account each month for the past year? Explain your answer.

   _____

   _____

2. What type of graph would you make to show the weight and length of a litter of kittens? Explain your answer.

   _____

   _____

3. Make a graph to show this data. Explain your choice of graph.

Trousers Fabric Content	
Polyester	53%
Wool	43%
Spandex	4%

   _____

   _____

4. Which graph would be best for comparing the average high and low temperatures for San Francisco each month of the year?

   A Double-bar graph   **C** Scattergram

   B Circle graph   **D** Double-line graph

5. **Writing to Explain** Linnea made a bar graph to show this data. Bobby made a circle graph. Which graph is appropriate for this data? Explain your reasoning.

Survey: How often do you go horseback riding	
Often	5
Sometimes	22
Never	83

   _____

   _____

   _____

Mean, Median, Mode, and Range

Find the mean, median, mode, and range of each data set. Round the decimal answers to the nearest hundredth.

1. 4, 6, 4, 5, 2, 3, 6, 7, 4 _____

2. 0.6, 0.9, 0.5, 0.3, 0.6, 0.4 _____

3. 32 mL, 42 mL, 88 mL, 35 mL, 40 mL, 73 mL, 88 mL, 17 mL

_____

4. If you told someone that the greatest depth in Lake Superior was 1,333 ft, would you be expressing a number similar to mode, median, mean, or range?

_____

_____

The chart shows the number of keys on several different kinds of musical instruments with keyboards.

5. To the nearest whole number, find the mean in the number of keys listed for each instrument.

_____

Instrument	Keys
Average spinet piano	88
Hammond organ	122
Clavichord	60
Harpsichord	48
Average grand piano	88

6. For this data set, which is greater, the median or the mode?

_____

7. The mean of a batting average of a baseball player for 5 years was .281. Four of his batting averages were .301, .299, .287, and .243. What was the fifth average?

   A .303   C .281

   B .286   D .275

8. **Writing to Explain** Sheila said that in any data set, the median and the mean are always very similar in value. Is she correct? Explain.

_____

_____

Frequency Tables and Histograms

Conrad recorded total the number of hours 14 friends spend on the Internet in a week. He made a frequency table of the data. Use the table for **1** through **2**.

Hours on the Internet	
Hours	**Frequency**
0–4	2
5–9	3
10–14	7
15–19	0
20–24	0
25–29	2

1. What is the mode of the data? Explain.

_____

_____

_____

2. How many friends spent 9 hours or less on the Internet that week?

_____

_____

Use the information below for **3** through **5**.

Ages of Players at Castle Miniature Golf				
14	7	6	24	15
9	19	25	10	17
51	8	21	48	12

Ages of Players at Castle Miniature Golf

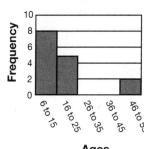

3. How many of the players are over 25? Explain.

_____

_____

4. Where do most of the data in the histogram cluster?

   A 6–15   **C** 26–55

   B 16–25   **D** Over 15

5. Writing to Explain Explain how you can tell whether a histogram has an outlier.

_____

_____

Stem-and-Leaf Plots

The chart at the right shows how far the girls in Shelly's Girl Scout troop could throw a softball.

Softball Throw Distance (ft)					
44	40	48	35	38	51
55	36	32	47	29	28
54	33	42	36	50	41

1. Represent the data as a stem-and-leaf plot.

2. Find the median, mode, and range of the data.

_____

The prices of items in dollars in two stores are displayed in the stem-and-leaf plots.

3. What is the range of prices for each store?

_____

4. Which store has the greater mean?

_____

Store 1	
Stem	**Leaves**
1	0 1 2 4
2	1 3 6 7 8
3	0 1 2 2 2 4 8
4	0 1 2 5

KEY: 1 | 0 = 10

Store 2	
Stem	**Leaves**
2	0 1 8 9 9
3	1 3 7 8
4	0 1 2 3 4 6 7 9
5	5 7 8

KEY: 1 | 0 = 10

5. Use the stem-and-leaf plots above. Which is the mode for Store 2?

   A $29   **C** $20

   B $21   **D** $9

6. Writing to Explain Explain what a store owner might learn by doing a stem-and-leaf plot of the prices of items in her store.

_____

_____

Appropriate Use of Statistical Measures

1. Find the mean, median, and mode of this data set:
   76, 74, 78, 72, 73, 80, 49, 72, 83

   _____

2. Which measure of central tendency best describes the data set? Why?

   _____

   _____

3. Find the mean, median, and mode of this data set:
   13, 19, 17, 15, 11, 19, 18

   _____

4. Which measure of central tendency best describes the data set? Why?

   _____

   _____

5. Find the mean, median, and mode of this data set:
   150, 138, 130, 127, 140, 108, 138

   _____

6. **Critical Thinking** What number could be added to the data set so that the mean, median, and mode are all the same?

   _____

7. **Writing to Explain** Ava found the mean, median, and mode of a data set. Then she discovered that she had not included a very high outlier in her calculations. How will the mean, median, and mode be affected by the inclusion of this outlier? Explain.

   _____

   _____

   _____

Samples and Surveys

In **1** and **2**, identify the population for the group studied. Then tell whether you think the data were drawn from a sample or an entire population. Explain your thinking.

1. A toy store found that 20% of its customers have grandchildren.

   _____

   _____

2. 12% of sixth-grade students at Perris Middle School are members of at least three clubs.

   _____

   _____

In **3** and **4,** explain why the sample is biased and how it could be fixed to be representative.

3. To find how many students in the school take music lessons, Emily surveyed 10 students in her home room. She found that 2% take music lessons.

   _____

   _____

4. Mr. Ellis wants to know how many students eat fruit at lunch. He polls every third student in the cafeteria line in one of two lunch periods.

   _____

   _____

   _____

5. A survey of members of a travel club shows that 35% prefer adventure packages. Which best describes the population of the survey?

   A People who prefer adventure packages when traveling

   B The members of a travel club who prefer adventure packages

   C All of the members of a travel club

   D People who travel

6. **Writing to Explain** The owner of a sandwich shop wants to know which sandwich special customers like best. Explain how the owner could take a survey to find out this information.

   _____

   _____

Using Statistics to Draw Conclusions

Name _____

Practice
19-10

Using Statistics to Draw Conclusions

1. Which question do you think is most fair? Explain.

   A Are you in favor of increasing speed limits on highways?

   B Is it safe to increase speed limits on highways?

   C Is it a good idea to have speed limits on highways?

   _____

   _____

Use the stem-and-leaf plot to draw conclusions about the ages of volunteers at an animal shelter.

Tell whether each claim is valid based on the stem-and-leaf plot. Explain your answer.

Ages of Volunteers

Stem	Leaf
1	6 6 8
2	3 8
3	0 3 4 6
4	2

KEY: 2|0 = 20

2. Volunteers are likely to be 35 or older.

   _____

3. 50% of the volunteers are younger than 29.

   _____

4. More teenagers volunteer than adults.

   _____

5. **Reasonableness** Suppose that the mean height of 14 girls on a basketball team is 63 inches. Which is a reasonable conclusion?

   A The mean height is greater than the median height.

   B 50% of the girls are taller than 63 inches.

   C The mode is 63 inches.

   D The mean height will increase if Mia who is 64 inches joins the team.

6. **Writing to Explain** A survey question asked: *Should students be required to learn a second language?* 11% said yes and 89% said no. Does the survey support the claim that most people do not want to learn a second language? Explain your thinking.

   _____

   _____

Problem Solving:
Try, Check, and Revise

1. The mean number of passengers on a daily flight from Los Angeles to San Francisco is 82. The plane holds a maximum of 102 passengers. List the possible number of passengers on the flight over the past 5 days.

_____

2. Four adult pandas weigh between 200 and 275 pounds. Their median weight is 240 pounds. List four possible weights for the pandas.

_____

3. Over the past 7 years the median rainfall in West Berry has been 74 inches. The greatest rainfall was 102 inches. The least was 52 inches. List possible rainfall amounts for the 7 years.

_____

4. The mean number of miles Mr. Austin drove in six days was 96. The mode was 82. The median was 97. What are possible distances Mr. Austin drove in the 6 days?

_____

5. **Writing to Explain** The mode of the heights of 5 sunflowers is 70 inches. The median is 68 inches. What are some possible heights of the 5 sunflowers? Tell how you decide.

_____

_____

_____

6. **Number Sense** Three consecutive odd integers have a sum of 195. What are the integers?

_____

7. **Geometry** The area of a rectangle is 180 square inches. The perimeter is 58 inches. What are the dimensions of the rectangle?

   A   30 in. by 6 in.   C   14 in. by 16 in.

   B   20 in. by 9 in.   D   12 in. by 15 in.

Counting Methods

1. Students can choose one sandwich, one fruit, and one drink. Make a tree diagram to show all the possible choices of a school lunch.

School Lunches

Sandwiches	Fruits	Drinks
Peanut butter	Apple	Milk
Tuna	Orange	Juice
	Banana	Water

_____

2. Show how you could use multiplication to find the outcome.

_____

Use any counting method you like.

3. How many possible outcomes are there if you spin each spinner once?

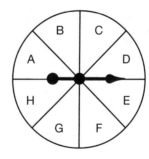 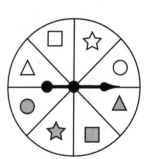

_____

4. Sandra has four color cards: one blue, one red, one green, and one yellow. If she puts them in a box, in how many different orders could she draw them out?

   A 16   **B** 24   **C** 32   **D** 64

5. **Writing to Explain** A basketball team needs 5 players. The team can choose from a group of 6 players. Explain how to find the number of combinations of players that can be on the team. How many combinations are there?

_____

Permutations and Combinations

Find the number of permutations or combinations. State whether it is a permutation or a combination.

1. A farmer has 4 horses that he wants to put into 4 different stalls. How many ways can he put them in the stalls?
   Think: __ × __ × __ × __ = ____

   _____

2. Paola has 10 bracelets. How many ways can she choose 2 of the bracelets to wear to a party? Think: How many pairs can she make from the 10 bracelets?

   _____

In **3** through **6**, find the number of possible arrangements and state whether it is a permutation or combination.

3. There are 8 games in a basketball tournament. Sal wants to watch 2 of the games. How many different ways can he watch the games?

   _____

4. Terri, Michael, Joshua, Brittany, Nina, Ty, Kelsie, and Jon play in a softball league. How many ways can they pair up to practice pitching and batting?

   _____

5. A lock has three dials with the digits 0 through 9. How many codes to open the lock are possible?

   _____

6. A car dealer received a shipment of 6 new truck models. How many ways can the dealer choose 2 of the models to put in the showroom?

   A 12 ways   **B** 15 ways   **C** 30 ways   **D** 720 ways

7. **Writing to Explain** Carlos has a 6-disc DVD player and he wants to load 6 DVDs in the player. Explain how he can determine the number of ways he can load the DVDs.

   _____

   _____

Probability

Use the spinner at the right. Find each probability as a fraction, decimal, and percent rounded to the nearest whole percent.

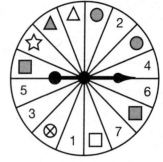

1. $P(\text{star})$ _____ ; _____ ; _____

2. $P(\text{shaded shape})$ _____ ; _____ ; _____

3. $P(\text{number})$ _____ ; _____ ; _____

In Exercises **4** and **5**, draw a set of 10 number cards that could yield each probability.

4. $P(4) = \frac{3}{10}$

5. $P(\text{odd number}) = 70\%$

6. A box holds 2 green cards, 3 blue cards, 7 orange cards, 1 red card, and 5 yellow cards. Which is **NOT** the probability that you will draw a blue card?

A $\frac{1}{6}$ **B** $\frac{3}{20}$ **C** 0.167   **D** 17%

7. Writing to Explain Corina said that she had a greater chance of getting heads on the second flip of a penny if the first flip was tails. Is she correct? Explain.

_____

_____

Theoretical and Experimental Probability

1. You have 26 number cards, numbered from 1 to 26. How many times might you expect to draw the 24 card in 1,300 tries?

   _____

2. If you had a jar with 166 white marbles and 2 red marbles, and you reached in without looking, how many times might you select a red marble after 1,000 tries?

   _____

3. **Reasoning** Gene said that if you toss a number cube 420 times, you will get a 1 about 70 times. Is he correct? Explain.

   _____

   _____

   _____

In baseball, a player's batting average is found by dividing the number of hits by the number of times he or she has been at bat. The batting average is therefore an expression of experimental probability.

4. Casey had 637 at bats last season, and he got hits on 213 of those at bats. What is the experimental probability that he will get a hit the next time he has an at bat?

   _____

5. Sam has a batting average of .346. How many base hits can he expect to get in 544 at bats?

   _____

6. A spinner has four sections of equal size: blue, green, yellow, and red. How many times might you expect to spin green out of 2,200 spins?

   A 500   **C** 700

   B 550   **D** 1000

7. **Writing to Explain** Explain how to find the experimental probability of getting heads in 100 coin flips.

   _____

   _____

   _____

Independent and Dependent Events

You select one letter card at random from these cards. You replace the letter card and select another.

| M | E | D | O | C | N | I | L |

1. Find P(consonant, consonant)

_____

2. Find P(consonant, vowel)

_____

3. Find P(vowel, N)

_____

4. Find P(consonant, O)

_____

5. Find P(vowel, vowel)

_____

6. Find P(N, O)

_____

You select one letter without looking, do not replace it, then select another. Give your answer as a percent, rounded to the nearest whole percent.

| P | Z | U | O | T | I | W | X | A | S |

7. Find P(consonant, vowel)

_____

8. Find P(vowel, vowel)

_____

9. Find P(vowel, Z)

_____

10. Find P(X, consonant)

_____

11. Find P(consonant, consonant)

_____

12. Find P(T, O)

_____

13. Jackie and two friends are drawing from a bag that contains savings cards for a popular store. There are twenty 10%-off cards, ten 15%-off cards, six 20%-off cards, and four 50%-off cards. What is the probability that Jackie will choose a 50%-off card as her third choice? Assume that her friends did not draw a 50%-off card.

A $\frac{1}{125}$

B $\frac{7}{625}$

C $\frac{2}{25}$

D $\frac{2}{19}$

Problem Solving:
Make an Organized List

Make an organized list to solve each problem.

1. Ernest is planting red, purple, yellow and white flowers. How many different ways can he plant the flowers in a row if the red and purple flowers are not next to each other?

_____

2. How many different combinations of baked goods can Jessie buy if she spends exactly $18?

Pies	$9 each
Cakes	$12 each
Bread	$3 loaf
Cookies	$1 each

_____

3. **Writing to Explain** How many different ways can 3 boys and 3 girls sit on these three stools if a boy does not sit next to a boy and a girl does not sit next to a girl. Explain how you decide.

_____

_____

4. **Number Sense** If you throw 3 darts at this dart board and hit it every time, how many different scores are possible?

A 6

B 9

C 10

D 15

5. The sixth graders are performing a play on Friday, Saturday, and Sunday. Each day there are performances at 4:00 PM, 6:00 PM, and 8:00 PM. How many possible choices for a day and time are there?

_____

6. In one town, the animal licenses have 3 different letters from the first 5 in the alphabet and 3 digits. How many possible choices for a pet's license are there?

_____